Más fácil

A Concise Review of Spanish Grammar

Estelita Calderón-Young
Collin County Community College

Rodney M. Mebane

Prentice Hall, Englewood Cliffs, New Jersey 07632

Library of Congress Cataloging-in-Publication Data

Calderón-Young, Estelita.
  Más fácil: a concise review of Spanish grammar / by Estelita
Calderón-Young, Rodney M. Mebane.
    p.   cm.
  Includes index.
  ISBN 0-13-178336-X
  1. Spanish language—Grammar—1950- —Handbooks, manuals, etc.
I. Mebane, Rodney M.   II. Title.
PC4112.C2   1993
468.2'421—dc20   92-35386
                                                            CIP

Executive Editor: *Steve Debow*
Associate Editor: *Tracey McPeake*
Editorial Assistant: *María García*
Cover Design: *Design Source*
Prepress Buyer: *Herb Klein*
Manufacturing Buyer: *Bob Anderson*

Printed in the United States of America

10 9 8 7 6 5 4 3 2

ISBN   0-13-178336-X

Prentice-Hall International (UK) Limited, *London*
Prentice-Hall of Australia Pty. Limited, *Sydney*
Prentice-Hall Canada Inc., *Toronto*
Prentice-Hall Hispanoamericana, S.A., *Mexico*
Prentice-Hall of India Private Limited, *New Delhi*
Prentice-Hall of Japan, Inc., *Tokyo*
Simon & Schuster Asia Pte. Ltd., *Singapore*
Editora Prentice-Hall do Brasil, Ltda., *Rio de Janeiro*

*This manual is dedicated to the women
who made the work possible:*

Ofelia F. Calderón, for her constant loving support,

*Barbara M. Mebane, Donna D. Mebane, and
Sarah E. Mebane, for their extraordinary
capacity to inspire.*

*T*able of *C*ontents

CHAPTER   5

Preface

The **Más fácil** project began in early 1990. At that time, we recognized the need for a complete, concise, and easy-to-use grammar review for students of Spanish. We believed that through a collaborative effort—combining our different experiences, perspectives, and talents—we could fill this important niche in a meaningful way. The volume you now hold, completed some three years after the project began, is the final result of this effort. We hope **Más fácil** advances your own educational interests in a significant way.

The book was developed for a variety of settings: as a recommended reference guide for beginning students or as a grammar review text for intermediate and advanced learners. Special attention was paid to using pedagogical devices designed for both the novice and the skilled student; and all explanations and examples were extensively reviewed and revised to appeal to today's English-speaking students of Spanish who may not be particularly proficient with grammar in their own native language. The book's tight organization, convenient format, and abundant tables will help such students get over the many hurdles that grammar can impose.

We owe gratitude to our editors, Steve Debow and Kristin Swanson, sources of much good advice and support, and to the following individuals who offered suggestions at various stages of development: Teresa Arrington, *University of Mississippi,* Douglas Benson, *Kansas State University,* Barbara Davis, *Onondaga Community College,* Guadalupe López-Cox, *Austin Community College,* Antonio Martínez, *University of Nebraska,* Lynn Carbón Gorrell, *The Pennsylvania State University,* William Clarkson, *San Antonio College,* and R. Alan Meredith, *Brigham Young University.*

At Hispanex, we extend our sincere appreciation to José A. Blanco, Pedro Urbina-Martin, Dana Slawsky, and Javier Amador-Peña, who guided the work through the editorial and technical production maze. At Prentice Hall, we thank Caroline Huber, who first "discovered" the **Más fácil** project, Jan Stephan, Alda Trabucchi, María García, and Rolando Hernández, each of whom has contributed ideas to the final publication.

Finally, for what seems like limitless indulgence throughout the book's development, we acknowledge, with love and gratitude, the support of all of our wonderful family members.

ECY
RMM

About the Authors

Estelita Calderón-Young, a native speaker of Spanish and an instructor of Spanish for the last eighteen years, was named in 1990 as the first full-time Professor of Spanish at the Collin County Community College (CCCC), serving communities north of Dallas, Texas, where she was named Outstanding Professor in 1991. Prior to joining the faculty of CCCC, Ms. Calderón-Young taught as an adjunct professor at Richland College in Dallas, where she was also recognized as the school's Outstanding Instructor in 1989. She is the 1992 recipient of the NISOD Excellence in Teaching Award and has recently been certified by ACTFL as one of the nation's select Oral Proficiency Testers. Ms. Calderón-Young lives in Garland, Texas, with her husband and three children.

Rodney M. Mebane is currently chief executive officer of Wordsmith Associates—a custom communications company, based in St. Charles, Illinois, offering specialized publication services to corporate and individual clients. During the development of **Más fácil**, Mr. Mebane served as treasurer for Southern Methodist University in Dallas, Texas. He earned his B.A. from Swarthmore College in 1974 and his M.A. from the University of Pennsylvania's Annenberg School of Communication in 1977. Mr. Mebane is broadly published in matters pertaining to investment, finance, and educational administration. He currently resides with his wife and four children in Geneva, Illinois.

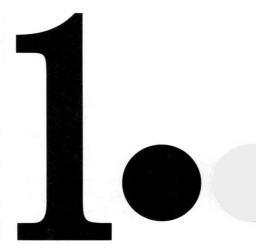

1 | *O*verview (ove)

As its name implies, **Más fácil** is designed to help students with the difficulties of Spanish grammar. Students at any level will benefit from **Más fácil's** consolidated format and innovative section reference system. **Más fácil** is so easy to use, it may make taking notes obsolete.

Learning a language requires three things: 1) the ability to speak and listen, 2) the ability to read and write, and 3) an understanding of the rules governing relationships among words. **Más fácil** is specifically written to clarify the technical grammatical difficulties of the Spanish language.

Más fácil is distinctive for two reasons:

- It is the most complete and compact grammar guide currently available anywhere. All rules and constructions needed for proficiency are included here, in fewer than 130 pages.

- It is specifically designed to simplify the tedious look-up process. For example, **Más fácil** enables a student to look up *quickly* the third person plural subject pronoun and the future tense forms of the verb **ser** *(to be)*—something that would be needlessly cumbersome with other texts.

It is important to recognize that **Más fácil** is intentionally written to supplement some other form of learning program. This allows **Más fácil** to include a massive amount of useful data—*without* a great deal of transitional text or fill-in-the-blank practice exercises. Instead, it provides dozens of easy-to-read tables, hundreds of carefully selected examples, full English-Spanish translations, and extensive cross-references.

Más fácil is arranged in eight sections. The first page of each section outlines its contents and directs the reader to subsections. The subsections are marked on the margin. (See example on this page.) The sections are as follows:

1. Getting Started
2. Nouns, Articles, & Adjectives
3. Pronouns, Adverbs, Interrogatives, Conjunctions, and Prepositions
4. Verbs
5. Functional Expressions
6. Appendix A: Glossary of English Grammar Terms
7. Appendix B: Glossary of Commonly Confused and Misused Terms
8. Appendix C: Conjugations of Thirty Common Verbs

This book is written for all students of Spanish. It is strongly recommended that users spend some time becoming familiar with the manual's material and layout. It should be an investment of time that pays off frequently.

Más fácil can also be used to remind native speakers and past students of Spanish of grammar rules. (It may also teach them a few things they do not already know.)

And to those altogether new to the language: Welcome. Learning a new language is difficult but very possible with real commitment. It is to your advantage that Spanish has many words that are very similar to English (**conversación**, for example). Also, the rules of Spanish grammar are quite consistent—there are relatively few "exceptions to the rule."

In general, if you are serious about learning Spanish, **Más fácil** will likely become **tu compañero** *(your companion)*. Please make it your own by marking it, adding to it, shaping it for your personal interests. And please let the authors know how **Más fácil** could be improved or extended. Language learning is an exciting, dynamic process, and we are all in it together.

2 | *Pronunciation* (pro)

In general, Spanish pronunciation is quite easy.

Virtually every letter in Spanish is pronounced, and the pronunciation of each letter, including vowels, is almost always the same. It behooves the student to learn the rules of pronunciation first. Once the student has learned these rules, effortless pronunciation follows. This helps to boost the learner's confidence and to ease the learning process dramatically.

Vowels and Diphthongs

The closest English equivalents to assist in the pronunciation of Spanish vowels are as follows:

a	—	ah	as in **pl*a*za**
e	—	eh	as in **caf*é***
i, y	—	e	as in **tort*i*lla**
o	—	o	as in **J*o*sé**
u	—	oo	as in **L*u*lu**[1]

Diphthongs result from the combinations of two vowels side by side. Of the vowels, there are three weak vowels, **i, y,** and **u,** and three strong vowels, **a, e,** and **o.** In Spanish, the diphthongs are pronounced as follows:

Weak — Weak	Pronounce both, emphasize the second vowel.
Weak — Strong Strong — Weak	} Pronounce both, emphasize the strong vowel.
Weak — Strong (with accent on weak) Strong — Strong	} Pronounce both, as two syllables.

---

[1] After **g** and **q**, the **u** is silent.

la ci*u***dad** city
acu*a***rio** aquarium
la fl*a***uta** flute

ego*í***sta** egotistical
distr*ae***r** distract

Consonants

In general, pronunciation of Spanish consonants is stronger and clearer than in English. However, a few consonants are pronounced more weakly than their English counterparts. These are **b** (and **v**), **d, g, p**, and **t.**

A complete guide to the pronunciation of consonants is provided on the next page.

The Alphabet[1]

The rules of pronunciation of vowels and consonants apply to the letters of the alphabet.

a	a	**k**	ka	**s**	ese
b	be, be grande[2]	**l**	ele	**t**	te
c	ce	**ll**[3]	elle	**u**	u
ch[3]	che	**m**	eme	**v**	ve, uve, ve
d	de	**n**	ene		chica[2]
e	e	**ñ**	eñe	**w**	uve doble, doble
f	efe	**o**	o		ve, doble u
g	ge	**p**	pe	**x**	equis
h	hache	**q**	cu	**y**	ye, igriega
i	i	**r**	ere	**z**	zeta
j	jota	**rr**[3]	erre		

Syllable Stress

As with punctuation, the rules of syllable stress are quite simple. There are only three.

1. When a word ends in a vowel, an **s**, or an **n**, the natural stress is on the next-to-last syllable:

---

[1] the letters of the alphabet are feminine.
[2] used to distinguish between **b** and **v** since they are pronounced similarly.
[3] alphabetized as a single letter.

CONSONANTS			
Letter	Condition	Closest English Sound	Example and Translation
b, v	Beginning of phrase, after **m** and **n**	Soft *b*	**Bien, gracias.** Fine, thanks.
	Between vowels	Weak *b*	**la prueba** test
	All other occurrences	*v*	**Está bien.** He is well.
c	Before **e** and **i**[1]	*s*	**la ciudad** city
	All other occurrences	*k*	**el campo** country
ch		*ch*	**el chicle** gum
d	Beginning of word, after **l** and **n**	*d*	**la democracia** democracy
	All other occurrences	Soft *d*	**pedir** to ask for
f		*f*	**el café** coffee
g	Before **e** and **i**	Harsh *h*	**Geraldo** Geraldo
	All other occurrences[2]	Soft *g*	**gracias** thanks
h	Not pronounced	—	**la hora** hour
j		*h*	**José** José
l		*l*	**libre** free
ll		*y*	**amarillo** yellow
m		*m*	**el semestre** semester
n	Before **m**, **b(v)**, and **p**	*m*	**inmediato** immediate
	All other occurrences	*n*	**la unidad** unity
ñ		*ny*	**la mañana** morning
p		*p*	**el español** Spanish
qu		*k*	**esquiar** to ski
r	Beginning of word	Trilled *r*	**la radio** radio
	Middle of word	*dd*	**el dinero** money
rr		Trilled *r*	**el perro** dog
s		*s*	**el sombrero** hat
t		*t*	**el tomate** tomato
x	Between vowels	*ks*	**el examen** examination
	Before a consonant	*s*	**la experiencia** experience
	In certain words	*h*	**Texas** Texas
y	Standing alone	Long *e*	**y** and
	All other occurrences	*y*	**leyendo** reading
z[1]		*s*	**la cerveza** beer

[1] In Spain, the letter **c** before **e** and **i** and the letter **z** on all occasions are pronounced as the English **th**.
[2] To keep the **g** sound, a **u** is inserted before **e** and **i**: **la guerra** *war*.

tra*b*ajo I work
no*s*otros we
es*m*oquin tuxedo

2.   Otherwise, the natural stress is on the last syllable:

liber*tad* liberty

3.   When the natural stress rules are not followed, an accent is required to indicate which syllable to stress.

bebé baby
canción song

Given these rules of placing emphasis, it can be observed that

*   a noun ending in **-ión** does not require an accent in the plural:

la acción action
las acciones actions

*   a noun ending in **-és** does not require an accent in the plural:

el interés interest
los intereses interests

*   a noun that does not require an accent in the singular may require one in the plural to maintain the same stressed syllable:

el orden order
los órdenes orders

Accents

In general, accents indicate the syllable to be stressed (as discussed above). In Spanish, therefore, there is never more than one accent in any single word. In addition, the accent is written in one direction only—from the lower left to the upper right.

When accents are *not* indicating stress, they are used to clarify the meaning of words that have the same spelling, as shown on the next page.

Accents Used to Distinguish Meaning

aún still	**aun** even	**sólo** only	**solo** alone
dé give	**de** of	**té** tea	**te** you
él he	**el** the	**tú** you	**tu** your
está he/she/it is	**ésta** this *(fem.)*		
mí me	**mi** my		
qué what	**que** that		
sí yes	**si** if		
sé I know	**se** self		

Accents are also used to distinguish question words (page 44) from their adverb counterparts in declarative statements.

3 | *Punctuation* (pun)

Punctuation Marks

, **coma** comma
; **punto y coma** semicolon
: **dos puntos** colon
. **punto final** period
... **puntos suspensivos** periods in a series
( ) **los paréntesis** parentheses
- **el guión** hyphen
— **la raya** dash
´ **acento escrito** accent mark
« » **las comillas** guillemets used in place of quotation marks
¿? **los signos de interrogación** question marks
¡! **los signos de admiración** exclamation marks
  (Question marks and exclamation marks are placed at the beginning and end of a partial or complete sentence.)
ñ **la tilde** accent (gives an **ny** sound as in *canyon*)
ü **la diéresis** diaeresis (indicates vowel that should be pronounced separately)

There is no use of the apostrophe in Spanish. See treatment of use of the preposition **de** to indicate possession on page 48.

Capitalization

Only the first word in a sentence and proper nouns are capitalized in Spanish.

Important differences:

- Days, months, etc., are not capitalized: **lunes** *Monday.*
- Countries are capitalized, nationalities and languages are not: **Francia** *France,* **francés** *French.*
- Religions are not capitalized: **católico** *Catholic.*
- Titles of individuals are not capitalized unless they are abbreviated: **señor García / Sr. García** *Mr. Garcia.*
- Titles of books, plays, etc., usually have only an initial capital: **Más fácil**.

3
pun

Other Rules of Punctuation

A comma is generally not used between the last two items in a series: **los caballos, las vacas y los puercos** *the horses, the cows, and the pigs.*

In Spanish, the use of commas and periods in numbers is reversed. The comma is used to indicate the decimals, while the period is used to separate thousands, millions, etc. For example, *100,000.00* would be written as 100.000,00.

Guillemets (foreign quotation marks) are used most often with a colon: **Él dijo: «Estoy muy cansado.»** *He said, "I'm very tired."*

In dialogue, direct quotations are generally indicated with dashes. Dashes are placed before and after the speech, thus indicating a break in the paragraph and identifying the speaker.

El joven vio a su novia en la joyería.	The young man saw his girlfriend in the jewelry store.
—¿Por qué estás aquí? —le dijo.	"Why are you here?" he said to her.
—¡Es un secreto! —ella respondió.	"It's a secret!" she replied.
—Estoy muy nervioso ahora...	"Now I am very nervous..."

4 | Structural Considerations (stc)

Spelling Observations and Word Endings

- **Double Letters**   With the exceptions of **ll**, **rr**, and **cc**, consonants are rarely doubled: *recommendation* → **recomendación**, *discussion* → **discusión**, *difference* → **diferencia**. The use of **cc** in Spanish often expresses the *ct* combination that is used in English: *perfection* → **perfección**.

- **The Letter Z**   The letter **z** cannot precede the letter **e** or **i** in Spanish. Instead, **z** changes to **c** before **e** and **i**: **la luz** *the light,* **las luces** *the lights.* This is why there is always a spelling change in the **yo** form of the preterite tense of a **-zar** verbs (page 91). **Comencé.** *I began.*

- **Prefixes**   The Spanish prefix **des-** can take the place of the English prefixes *dis, un-,* and *in-*. For example, the Spanish word for *inequality* is **desigualdad**.

  Generally, where the English *un-* is used, **in-** is used in Spanish: **insociable**. Where the English prefix *imm-* is used, **inm-** is used in Spanish: **inmediato**.

- **Diminutive Suffixes**   Making Something Smaller

  -ito(a), -cito(a) casa → **casita** *little house*
  -illo(a), -cillo(a) pan → **panecillo** *roll*
  -ico niño → **niñico** *little boy*

- **Augmentative Suffixes**   Making Something Bigger

  -ón camisa → **camisón** *nightgown (big shirt)*
  -azo(a) boca → **bocaza** *big mouth*
  -ote libro → **librote** *big book*

  (Note: Words with **-ote** endings are often depreciative or derogatory in meaning.)

• **Common Word Endings**   Many words in Spanish are cognates, similar to their English counterparts with just a change in word ending. Some common cognate endings are listed below, with examples.

-aire	**-ario**	**cuestion*ario***
-ary	**-ario**	**legend*ario***
-ble	**-ble**	**imposi*ble***
-ial	**-ial**	**imparc*ial***
-ian	**-io**	**humanitar*io***
-ile	**-il**	**infant*il***
-ion	**-ión**	**descripc*ión***
-ional	**-ional**	**nac*ional***
-ious	**-iente**	**inconsc*iente***
-ism	**-ismo**	**alcohol*ismo***
-ist	**-ista**	**especial*ista***
-ive	**-iva**	**iniciat*iva***
-ive	**-ivo**	**explos*ivo***
-logical	**-lógico**	**tecno*lógico***
-logy	**-logía**	**ideo*logía***
-ly	**-mente**	**adecuada*mente***
-nce	**-ncia**	**viole*ncia***
-ncy	**-ncia**	**urge*ncia***
-nt	**-nte**	**impacie*nte***
-ory	**-orio**	**direct*orio***
-ous	**-oso**	**delici*oso***
-phy	**-fía**	**fotogra*fía***
-ture	**-tura**	**litera*tura***
-ty	**-dad**	**reali*dad***
-ual	**-uo**	**individ*uo***
-ute	**-uto**	**instit*uto***
-y	**-ia**	**frecuenc*ia***
-y	**-ía**	**democrac*ía***
-y	**-io**	**remed*io***

4
stc

OTHER COMMON SUFFIXES

-er	**-ero(a)**	**curand*ero*** faith-heal*er*
-or	**-or(a)**	**embajad*or*** ambassad*or*
-ful	**-ada**	**cuchar*ada*** spoon*ful*
-store	**-ería**	**libr*ería*** book*store*

Contractions

to the...   **a + el = al**

Voy *al* lago.   I'm going *to the* lake.

of the, from the...   **de + el = del**

pescado *del* río   fish *from the* river

✌ Note

> **Al**, with an infinitive, is used to express *upon* or *after*.
>
> **Al escuchar al cura...**   *Upon* listening to the
>   priest...
>
> If **el** is part of a title of a work, there is no contraction:
>
> **Estoy cansado de *El***   I am tired of *The Captain.*
> ***capitán*.**

Word Order

In statements, the subject generally precedes the verb.

La *casa* está limpia.   The *house is* clean.

In questions, the subject often follows the verb.

¿Cómo esta *usted?*   How are *you?*

Descriptive adjectives (page 24) generally follow the noun they modify.

el camión *rojo*   the *red* truck

Limiting adjectives (page 25) generally precede the noun they modify.

Hay *doce* estudiantes en la clase.	There are *twelve* students in the class.

Pronouns generally come before the verb.

***Te* amo.**	I love *you*.

If an adverb is modifying a verb, it generally follows the verb.

Tú necesitas venir *pronto*.	You need to come *quickly*.

If an adverb is modifying an adjective, it generally precedes the adjective.

Estoy *muy* alegre esta mañana.	I am *very* happy this morning.

To make a sentence negative, the word **no** is placed before the conjugated verb.

***No* voy a la fiesta esta noche.**	I am *not* going to the party to-night.

Also see discussion of word order in connection with individual parts of speech.

4
stc

CHAPTER 2

5 Nouns

6 Articles

7 Adjectives
Descriptive Adjectives
Limiting Adjectives
Adjectives Used as Nouns
Other Adjective Considerations
Specific Types of Adjectives
Possessive Adjectives (see page 34)
Relative Adjectives (see page 41)

5 | *Nouns* (nou)

All nouns in Spanish have gender. That is, they are either *masculine* or *feminine*. All nouns in Spanish also denote number—singular (one referent) or plural (more than one referent).

The gender and number of Spanish nouns are generally indicated in combination with a *definite article,* which is equivalent to the English word *the (the book).* They can also be distinguished by an *indefinite article,* equivalent to the English words *a (a book)* and *some (some books).* There are four definite articles *(el, la, los, las)* and four indefinite articles *(un, una, unos, unas),* which correspond to the gender and number of the nouns they accompany (see page 19).

In the absence of an identifying article, the gender of a noun can often, but not always, be determined by its word ending. The following ten guidelines address most situations.

1.   Most masculine nouns end in **-o**.

     el puerto port
     el insecto insect

2.   Similarly, most feminine nouns end in **-a**.

     la historia history
     la vista view

3.   However, there are some masculine nouns ending in **-a**.

el clima climate	**el poeta** poet
el día day	**el problema** problem
el drama drama	**el programa** program
el idioma language	**el sistema** system
el mapa map	**el tema** theme

4. There are also a few feminine nouns ending in **-o**.

> **la foto**[1] photo
> **la mano** hand
> **la moto**[1] motorcycle

☞ Note

There are a few feminine nouns that begin with the stressed **a** sound. These require the singular **el** or **un**, normally associated with masculine nouns, and the feminine plural articles **las** or **unas**.

	Stressed:		
	el **agua** water	*las* **aguas**	
	el **águila** eagle	*las* **águilas**	
	un **alma** soul	*unas* **almas**	
	un **arma** firearm	*unas* **armas**	
	el **hacha** axe	*las* **hachas**	
	el **hambre** hunger	*las* **hambres**	

Unstressed: *la* **amiga** friend   *las* **amigas**

(See discussion of syllable stress on page 5.)

5. Nouns ending in **-dor** and **-sor,** usually equivalent to the English *-er* or *-or*, are generally masculine, with the feminine formed simply by adding an **-a**.

> **el trabaja*dor*** male work*er*
> **la trabaja*dora*** female work*er*

Other common feminine endings:

6. Nouns with the endings **-dad** and **-tad**, generally equivalent to the English *-ty,* are always feminine.

> **la ciu*dad*** ci*ty*
> **la dificul*tad*** difficul*ty*

---

[1] These result from shortening longer words (**fotografía, motocicleta**).

7. Nouns with the following endings are almost always feminine.

-d	**la pare**d wall
-tud	**la acti**tud attitude
-ión	**la conversa**ción conversation
-umbre	**la muched**umbre crowd
-ie	**la espe**cie species

8. Some nouns with the same spelling can be either masculine or feminine, depending on their meaning.

el capital money
el corte cut
el cura priest
el guía male guide
el policía male officer
el radio radio (physical object)
la capital capital city
la corte court
la cura cure
la guía guidebook, female guide
la policía police force, female officer
la radio radio station

9. Some other nouns with the same spelling can be either masculine or feminine, depending on the person to whom they refer.

el artista male artist
el estudiante male student
el joven young man
el novelista male novelist
la artista female artist
la estudiante female student
la joven young woman
la novelista female novelist

10. Finally, nouns ending in **-e, -s,** or other consonants vary in gender and must simply be memorized.

el coche car	**la leche** milk
el nombre name	**la clase** class
el autobús bus	**la crisis** crisis
el paraguas umbrella	**la tesis** thesis
el papel paper	**la cárcel** jail
el rincón corner	**la comezón** itch

The rules for making nouns plural are straightforward. If the singular noun ends in:

a vowel[1]	add **-s**	**el perro** dog	**los perros**
a consonant	add **-es**	**la pared** wall	**las paredes**
an **-s**	keep as is	**el lunes** Monday	**los lunes**
a **-z**	change **to c**, add **-es**	**el lápiz** pencil	**los lápices**

(For a discussion of nouns and accents, see page 7. For a discussion of pronunciation, see page 4.)

6 | *Articles* (art)

As mentioned in the introduction to nouns (page 16), there are various definite and indefinite articles in Spanish.

		DEFINITE ARTICLES		INDEFINITE ARTICLES	
Noun: Gender / Number		Singular	Plural	Singular	Plural
Masculine		**el**	**los**	**un**	**unos**
Feminine		**la**	**las**	**una**	**unas**

There is also a neuter article **lo**, used in special situations. See page 23.

---

[1] except for accented vowels or vowels ending in **-y**, where **-es** is added.

    el rubí ruby   **los rubíes**
    el rey king   **los reyes**

One of the most basic rules in Spanish is that an article must agree in gender and number with the noun identified, as follows:

el chico the boy	**los chicos** the boys
la ola the wave	**las olas** the waves
un rancho a ranch	**unos ranchos** some ranches
una familia a family	**unas familias** some families

In Spanish, the definite article plays a much more active role than in English. Uses of the definite article are described on the next page.

Regarding the indefinite article, there are certain situations in Spanish where an article is not included, when in English one normally would be.

Generally, indefinite articles are *not* used in the following six situations.

1. After a form of the verb **ser** *(to be)* when the noun following is *not* modified:

    Él es amigo.   He is *a* friend.

2. With a noun of rank, profession, religion, or nationality when such noun is *not* modified:

    Visité dentista.   I visited *a* dentist.

3. After the verbs **buscar** *(to look for)*, **encontrar** *(to meet)*, and **tener** *(to have)* where the number is implied:

    Busco trabajo.   I am looking for *a* job.

4. After the words **con** *(with)* and **sin** *(without)*:

    Sin duda está ya en   Without *a* doubt, she is already
    casa.   home.

5. With the Spanish words **cierto(a)** *(certain)*, **tal** *(such a)*, and **otro(a)** *(another)*:

    Leí otro libro.   I read *an*other book.
    No creerá tal cuento.   He will not believe such *a* story.

6. With the numbers **cien** *(100)* and **mil** *(1000)*:

> **Te debo cien dólares.**   I owe you *a* hundred dollars.

ᷛ **Note**

> Omission of the indefinite article after **ser** and in these other situations is because number is unimportant. The noun acts as a mere category for classification. However, if number is referred to specifically, for emphasis or to modify the noun, an article *must* be used.
>
> **Sólo tengo *una* hija.**   I have only one daughter.

6
art

Definite articles are used in the following fourteen situations.

1. With infinitives used as nouns (the gerund equivalent—page 85), particularly at the beginning of a sentence:

> ***El* esquiar es divertido.**   Skiing is fun.

2. With nouns in a series:

> **Traiga *el* libro, *el* lápiz   Bring the book, the pencil, and
> y *el* papel.**   the paper.

3. With feminine nouns that begin with the stressed **a** sound (page 17):

> ***El* agua está fría.**   The water is cold.

4. To identify an intangible concept:

> ***La* belleza es efímera.**   Beauty is ephemeral.

5. To identify a specific thing that is followed by a demonstrative adjective (page 29):

> ***la* chica ésta**   this girl

6. To express time of day (page 96):

      Voy a clase a *las* ocho   I go to class at 8:30.
      y media.

7. With days of the week to express *on,* except after **ser** (page 99):

      Fui al médico *el* lunes.   I went to the doctor on Monday.

8. With seasons of the year (page 100) when discussing a season in a general manner:

      Quiero ir a México en   I want to go to Mexico in the
      ***el* verano.**   summer.

9. With parts of the body (page 104) and personal expressions, to convey the meaning of a possessive pronoun:

      Me lavo *los* dientes.   I brush my teeth.
      Se pusieron *los*   They put on their shoes.
      zapatos.

10. Before the names of languages (except after **hablar, de,** or **en**):

      ***El* español es un**   Spanish is a beautiful lan-
      idioma bonito.   guage.

11. With proper names when modified:

      ***la* Inglaterra antigua**   old England
      ***la* pequeña María**   little Maria

12. With weights and measurements (to express *per*—page 102):

      Es solamente dos   It's only two pesos per kilo.
      pesos *el* kilo.

13. With the names of meals:

      Prefiero *el* desayuno   I prefer a complete breakfast.
      completo.

6
art

14. With titles, ranks, and professions when speaking about *(not to)* a person (page 9) and when the name of the person is included:

> ***La* señora de Martínez vino ayer.**   Mrs. Martínez came yesterday.
>
> ***El* doctor Álvarez es muy simpático.**   Dr. Álvarez is very pleasant.

The Neuter Article *Lo*

The neuter article **lo** *(it)* is used with a singular masculine form of a nominalized adjective (adjective used as a noun—page 27). It is also used to express an abstract idea or quality that is neither masculine nor feminine.

> **lo difícil** the difficult part
> **lo moderno** the modern thing
> **lo misterioso** the mysterious

In addition, it is also used in combination with the relative pronouns **que** and **cual** to say *that which* or *what* (page 41):

> **Él no sabe *lo que* quiere.**   He does not know *what* he wants.

7 | *Adjectives* (adj)

Like articles (page 20), adjectives must agree in gender and number with the nouns they modify. This agreement generally is in the form of the adjective ending.

> **el niño buen*o*** the good boy
> **la casa blanc*a*** the white house
> **los niños buen*os*** the good boys
> **las casas blanc*as*** the white houses

MOST COMMON ADJECTIVE ENDINGS		
	Singular	Plural
Masculine	**-o**	**-os**
Feminine	**-a**	**-as**

Certain adjectives in the masculine singular form end in **-dor**. In such cases, the feminine singular form is constructed by adding an **-a**.

un ambiente *acogedor* a *friendly* atmosphere (masculine)
la casa *acogedora* a *friendly* house (feminine)

Other adjectives ending in a consonant or in **-e** maintain the same form for both masculine and feminine nouns.

un trabajador *joven* the *young* (male) worker
la cantora *joven* the *young* (female) singer
el hombre *alegre* the *happy* man
una muchacha *alegre* the *happy* girl

The same rules apply to plural adjectives as to plural nouns (page 19). If the adjective ends in:

a vowel	add **-s**	**rico**	rich	**ricos**
a consonant	add **-es**	**fácil**	easy	**fáciles**
an **-s**	add **-es**	**gris**	gray	**grises**
a **-z**	change to **c**, add **-es**	**feliz**	happy	**felices**

Descriptive Adjectives

Most adjectives are descriptive in nature, telling some characteristic of the noun. In Spanish, descriptive adjectives generally follow the noun.

la chica *alta* the tall girl
el chico *guapo* the handsome boy

Exceptions:

1.   The adjective **lindo** *(pretty)* can go before or after the noun.

> la *linda* noche   the *pretty* night
> la muchacha *linda*   the *pretty* girl

2.   The adjectives **bueno** *(good)* and **malo** *(bad)* can also go before a noun, but the **-o** is dropped before a masculine singular noun.

> una *buena* razón   a *good* reason
> el *mal* olor   the *bad* smell

3.   The adjective **grande** *(big)* can go before or after, but changes to **gran** before nouns of either gender. When placed before a noun, **gran** means *great*. After a noun, **grande** means *large*. (**Grandes** is the plural form in either case.)

> **Fue un *gran* hombre.**   He was a *great* man.
> **Quiero una muñeca**   I want a *big* doll.
> *grande*.

7
adj

4.   Some adjectives change the meaning of the noun when placed before or after it. If after a noun, the adjective distinguishes the noun from others of the same class.

> **un hombre *pobre***   an *impoverished* man
> **una falda *nueva***   a *new (never before worn)* skirt

Before a noun, the adjective denotes inherent quality.

> **un *pobre* hombre**   an *unfortunate* man
> **una *nueva* falda**   a *new (different)* skirt

5.   Adjectives of nationality always follow the noun.

> **el vestido *mexicano***   the *Mexican* dress
> **la comida *china***   the *Chinese* food

Limiting Adjectives

Instead of being descriptive, many adjectives tell something about the limits of nouns, indicating number, quantity, or amount.

Limiting adjectives precede the noun.

> ***poca* gente** *few* people
> ***mucha* neblina** *much* fog

However, there are other conditions to keep in mind.

1. Possessive adjectives generally precede the noun, unless they are stressed in meaning.

***Mis* hijos son inteligentes.**	My children are intelligent.
Los hijos *míos* son inteligentes.	*My* children are intelligent.

2. If an exact number is used, the article is dropped.

   cinco caballos five horses

3. Like **bueno** and **malo**, the number-related adjectives **uno** *(one)*, **primero** *(first),* and **tercero** *(third)* are apocopated (they drop the **-o**) before masculine singular nouns.

   el *tercer* libro the *third* book
   mi *primer* novio my *first* boyfriend

4. **Alguno** *(some)* and **ninguno** *(none)* drop the **-o** before masculine singular nouns and add an accent over the **u**. (For a discussion of accents, see page 7.)

   Algún niño perdió esto.   *Some* child lost this.

5. The adjective **ciento** *(hundred)* changes to **cien** before all nouns as well as the words *thousand* and *million,* but no other numerals.

   ciento cinco 105
   cien mil 100.000

Note that in Spanish, instead of a comma, the period is used in numbers to indicate units of thousand. See a discussion of numbers on page 101.

Adjectives Used As Nouns

In Spanish, adjectives can be used as nouns. In English, the pronoun *one* is placed after the adjective to create a noun phrase *(the red **one**, some pretty **ones**, these strong **ones**)*. In Spanish, however, the adjective is preceded by a definite or indefinite article (page 19) or by a demonstrative adjective (page 29) in order to create an adjective phrase—**la roja**, **unas bonitas**, **estos fuertes**. This adjective phrase is used as a noun.

Nominalized adjectives (adjectives used as nouns) are also found in descriptive phrases using **de** *(of)*—see page 48.

    una *de* algodón a cotton one

Note that if the indefinite article for *one* is used with a masculine singular reference, **uno** should be used, not **un**:

    ***uno* triste** *a sad* one

**7
adj**

Other Adjective Considerations

1. If both a descriptive and a limiting adjective are used, place the descriptive after the noun, and the limiting before.

        muchas* mujeres *bonitas *many beautiful* women

2. If an adjective follows a masculine and a feminine noun, the masculine plural form is used.

        la mesa y el libro *amarillos* the *yellow* table and the *yellow* book

3. If an adjective precedes a masculine and a feminine noun, it should agree with the closest noun.

        ***muchos* hombres y mujeres** *many* men and women

4. If two or more adjectives follow a noun, the Spanish word **y** *(and)* is generally used before the last adjective.

        el hombre rico, moreno *y* guapo the rich, dark, handsome man

Note that in Spanish, a comma is *not* used between the last and next-to-last adjectives in a series. See a discussion on punctuation on page 9.

Specific Types of Adjectives

Past Participles

In many cases, the past participle form of a verb (page 82) is used as a descriptive adjective. These generally end in **-ado** and **-ido** and are equivalent to the English *-ed* form.

> **asustar** to scare   **asustado** scared
> **encantar** to delight   **encantado** delighted

7 adj

Adjectives of Nationality

All adjectives of nationality, descriptive in nature, have four forms like all other adjectives, corresponding to the gender and number of the noun they modify (or take the place of), as shown.

	MASCULINE FORM ENDING IN **-O**		MASCULINE FORM ENDING IN CONSONANT	
	Mexican		*Spanish*	
Masculine	**mexicano**	**mexicanos**	**español**	**españoles**
Feminine	**mexicana**	**mexicanas**	**española**	**españolas**

Note that the first letter of an adjective of nationality is *not* capitalized. Only the names of countries themselves are capitalized (page 9).

For a listing of different countries and nationalities, see page 104.

DEMONSTRATIVE ADJECTIVES			
Agreeing in gender and number:	*Masculine*	*Feminine*	*Related Adverb*
this these	**este** **estos**	**esta** **estas**	**aquí** *(here)*
that those	**ese** **esos**	**esa** **esas**	**ahí** *(there)*
that distant those distant	**aquel** **aquellos**	**aquella** **aquellas**	**allí** *(over there)*

7 adj

Generally, the demonstrative adjective precedes the noun it modifies (*esta* **vida** *this* life). If it follows, a definite article is required (*la* **vida** *esta*).

If the demonstrative adjective is nominalized (used as a demonstrative pronoun), an accent is normally placed over the (initial) **é**.

Va a comprar *esa* casa.   He is going to buy *that* house.
Va a comprar *ésa*.   He is going to buy *that one*.

These are common in the beginning of sentences.

***Éste* es el mío.**   *This one* is mine.

Aquél is used to express *the former*.

De los dos planes,   Of the two ideas, I prefer *the*
prefiero *aquél*.   *former*.

A complete listing of demonstrative pronouns may be found on page 40.

Ordinals: The Number Adjectives

Ordinals are a form of limiting adjectives (page 25) and should always agree in gender and number.

primero[1]	first	**sexto**	sixth
segundo	second	**séptimo**	seventh
tercero[1]	third	**octavo**	eighth
cuarto	fourth	**noveno**	ninth
quinto	fifth	**décimo**	tenth

Primero is often indicated as 1°.

1° de abril April 1st

Ordinals are rarely used beyond ten. Instead, the number is used and it follows the noun.

el piso *quince* the *15th* floor

**7
adj**

---

[1] drop the **-o** before a masculine singular noun

    su *primer* niño her *first* son

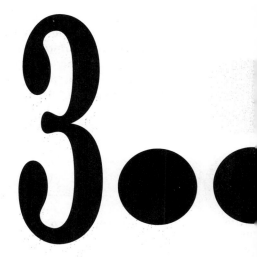

8 | *Pronouns* (prn)

There are more pronouns in Spanish than in English. In Spanish, they have many functions and are used extensively. The various pronoun forms, along with their English translations and examples of their use, are detailed on the following pages.

Subject Pronouns

Used to indicate the subject of the sentence:

	Singular	*Plural*
1st person	**yo** I	**nosotros(as)** we
2nd person	**tú** you (familiar)	**vosotros(as)** you
3rd person	**él**, **ella**, **usted*** he, she, you (formal)	**ellos(as)**, **ustedes*** they, you

* The second person formal subject pronouns **usted** and **ustedes** may also be abbreviated **Ud.** and **Uds.**, always capitalized.

There are subject pronouns for people but not for things.

Spanish verb endings reveal the subject, and thus the use of subject pronouns is often optional. Subject pronouns are used, however, for clarity, emphasis, and courtesy.

Tú **comes mucho.**	*You* eat a lot.
Comes mucho.	You eat a lot.

Subject pronouns are also necessary when a clause is without a verb.

Ellos van a España, pero *nosotros* **no.**	They are going to Spain, but *we* are not.

They are used after the verb **ser** *(to be)*.

¿Quién es el profesor de esta clase? Soy *yo.*	Who is the professor of this class? *I* am.

Prepositional Pronouns

Used after prepositions:

	Singular	*Plural*
1st Person	**mí** me	**nosotros(as)** us
2nd Person *(fam.)*	**ti** you	**vosotros(as)** you
3rd Person, 2nd *(form.)*	**él, ella, usted** him/ her/you	**ellos(as), ustedes** them/you

El café es para *mí.*	The coffee is for *me*.

Note that there is also the form **sí** used to mean *himself, herself, yourself, themselves, yourselves*. These pronouns, with **sí** used in the third person, also serve as prepositional pronouns in reflexive situations (page 80).

After the preposition **con**, singular pronouns change to a compound form.

conmigo	**Venga** *conmigo.* Come *with me.*
contigo	**Fue** *contigo.* He went *with you.*
consigo *(reflexive)*	**¿Lo trae** *consigo?* Do you have it *with you?*

Possessive or Adjective Pronouns

Used as adjectives before nouns:

	Singular	Plural
1st Person	**mi(s)** my	**nuestro(a/os/as)** our
2nd Person *(fam.)*	**tu(s)** your	**vuestro(a/os/as)** your
3rd Person, 2nd *(form.)*	**su(s)** his/her/your	**su(s)** their, your

Esta es *tu* vida.   This is *your* life.

Used as adjectives after or in place of nouns:

	Singular	Plural
1st Person	**mío(a/os/as)** mine	**nuestro(a/os/as)** ours
2nd Person *(fam.)*	**tuyo(a/os/as)** yours	**vuestro(a/os/as)** yours
3rd Person, 2nd *(form.)*	**suyo(a/os/as)** his/ hers/yours	**suyo(a/os/as)** theirs/ yours

When adjective pronouns are used in the place of nouns (nominalized), they are accompanied by a definite article (page 19), except after the verb **ser,** when the definite article is omitted.

Possessive pronouns must agree in gender and number with the nouns they modify.

Allí están *tus* hijos.
¿Dónde están los *míos?*
Ésta es *mi* tarea, ésa es tuya.

There are *your* children. Where are *mine?*
This is *my* homework, that is *yours.*

The possessive adjective **cuyo(a/os/as),** agreeing in gender and number, refers to a noun antecedent and means *whose* or *of whom.*

El hombre, en *cuya* oficina...

The man, in *whose* office...

Reflexive Pronouns

Used with reflexive verbs, when the action is done to oneself:

	Singular	*Plural*
1st Person	**me** myself	**nos** ourselves
2nd Person *(fam.)*	**te** yourself	**os** yourselves
3rd Person, 2nd *(form.)*	**se** himself/herself/ yourself	**se** themselves, yourselves

Me afeitaré en la mañana.   I will shave (myself) in the morning.

Generally, reflexive pronouns precede verbs.

Me duele la cabeza.   My head hurts.

However, the pronoun may attach to an affirmative command, an infinitive, or a present participle.

Lávate.	Wash yourself.
Vamos a irnos.	We are going to leave.
Está bañándose.	She's bathing.

With compound verb forms, the pronoun may precede the conjugated verb.

| **Nos vamos a ir.** | We are going to leave. |
| **Se está bañando.** | She's bathing. |

To form a negative reflexive pronoun sentence, the word **no** is placed before the reflexive pronoun.

Yo *no* me retiraré este año.   I will not retire this year.

Reflexive pronouns become reciprocal pronouns when the action described is not a direct action done to oneself, but is a reciprocal action done by two or more people to each other at the same time.

Se **besan.**   They kiss (each other).

Direct Object Pronouns

Used in place of direct object nouns:

	Singular	*Plural*
1st Person	**me** me	**nos** us
2nd Person *(fam.)*	**te** you	**os** you
3rd Person, 2nd	**lo, le*** him/you (m.)/it	**los (las)** them/
(form.)	**la** her/you (f.)/it	you

* Note that in some areas, **le** is used instead of **lo**. Because **lo** and **los** also serve as the neuter referents, they are called the impersonal direct object pronouns.

Lo **busco.**   I am looking for *it.*
Te **busco.**   I am looking for *you.*
Las **busco.**   I am looking for *them.*

In negative sentences, the word **no** precedes the object pronoun.

No **lo busco.**   I am *not* looking for it.

With commands, direct object pronouns attach to affirmative commands and precede negative ones.

¡**Bése***lo* **ahora!**   Kiss *him* now!
¡**No** *lo* **bese nunca!** Don't kiss *him* ever!

Direct object pronouns attach to infinitives and present participles.

Voy a mirar*lo.*   I am going to watch *it.*
Estoy mirándo*lo.*   I am watching *it.*

Or they may precede the conjugated verb.

***Lo* voy a mirar.**   I am going to watch *it.*

Indirect Object Pronouns

Used to indicate to whom or for whom something is done or to indicate who or what is affected by the action.

	Singular	*Plural*
1st Person	**me** me	**nos** us
2nd Person *(fam.)*	**te** you	**os** you
3rd Person, 2nd *(form.)*	**le*** him/her/you/it	**les*** them/you

* **Le** and **les** change to **se** when combined with a direct object pronoun (page 39). If there is any doubt regarding the referent of **le, les,** or **se,** include a prepositional phrase—**a** + the appropriate prepositional pronoun (page 33)—after the conjugated verb.

8
prn

Consuelo le canta *a él.***   Consuelo is singing *to him.*
(A Carlos) *le* dieron un regalo.   They gave a present *to him* (Carlos).

When the construction calls for it, as in the examples above, an indirect object pronoun is required even if the person/thing being referred to is included in the sentence. Note that the personal **a** is used to clarify the referent (see page 47).

Like direct object pronouns, indirect object pronouns attach to affirmative commands and precede negative ones.

Díga*me* la verdad.   Tell *me* the truth.
No *me* diga la verdad.   Don't tell *me* the truth.

Indirect object pronouns may attach to infinitives and present participles.

Voy a decir*le.***   I am going to tell *her.*
Estoy esperándo*te.***   I am expecting *you.*

Or they may precede the conjugated verb.

Le **voy a decir.**	I am going to tell *her.*
Te **estoy esperando.**	I am expecting *you.*

Indirect object pronouns are used with a number of verbs where *to someone* is suggested.

asustar to be scary to
bastar to be enough to
encantar to be enchanting to
enfurecer to be infuriating to
enojar to be annoying to
faltar to be lacking to
fascinar to be fascinating to
gustar to be pleasing to
hacer falta to be necessary to
importar to be important to

interesar to be interesting to
llamar la attención to call attention to
parecer to appear to
pasar to happen to
placer to be pleasing to
quedar to be left to
sorprender to be surprising to
tocar to be touching to

A special class of these is referred to as the information verbs because, in communication, *to someone* is also implied.

cantar to sing (to)
contestar to answer (to)
decir to tell (to)
escribir to write (to)

explicar to explain (to)
hablar to speak (to)
informar to report (to)
preguntar to ask (of)

Me **contó un chiste.**	He told me a joke.
Le **contestó al profesor en español.**	She answered the professor in Spanish.

Indirect object pronouns are also used with personal expressions, to indicate possession.

Nos **limpia la ropa.**	He is cleaning *our* clothes *(for us).*

They are used with impersonal expressions.

Le **es necesario salir.**	It is necessary *for him* to leave.

Indirect and Direct Object Pronouns

Step 1. **Carlos está comprando**   Carlos is buying the book for *us.*
el libro para *nosotros.*
(prepositional pronoun)

Step 2. **Carlos está comprán-**   Carlos is buying *it* for us.
do*lo* para nosotros.
(direct object pronoun)

Step 3. **Carlos *nos* está com-**   Carlos is buying (for) *us* the
prando el libro. (in-   book.
direct object pronoun)

Step 4. **Carlos está comprán-**   Carlos is buying *us it.*
do*noslo.* (indirect and
direct object pronouns)

Note that when used together, indirect object pronouns always precede the direct object pronouns.

Special Uses of the Pronoun *Se*

Le and **les**, the third person indirect object pronouns, change to **se** when used in combination with direct object pronouns.

Si le falta dinero,   If he needs money, I can give *it*
puedo dár*selo.*   *to him.*

***Se los* di esta mañana.**   I gave *them to him* this morning.
Dé*selo.*   Give *it to him.*

Se is also used as an impersonal pronoun to express the passive voice (page 81). It is used in the form of:

se + *3rd person form of verb* + *performer or recipient of action*

***Se* espera lluvia.**   Rain is expected.
En este restaurante *se*   Rice is served in this restau-
sirve arroz.   rant.
No *se* permite pescar   Fishing is not allowed here.
aquí.

Demonstrative Pronouns

Demonstrative pronouns change according to the gender and number of the nouns they replace.

	Masculine	Feminine	Neuter
this	**éste**	**ésta**	**esto**
these	**éstos**	**éstas**	**estos**
that	**ése**	**ésa**	**eso**
those	**ésos**	**ésas**	**esos**
that (distant)	**aquél**	**aquélla**	**aquello**
those (distant)	**aquéllos**	**aquéllas**	**aquellos**

To avoid confusion, the masculine and feminine demonstrative pronouns, when used as adjectives, do not have accents (page 29). The neuter forms do not have accents; since they are not used as adjectives, there is no confusion.

8
prn

Este chico quiere este juguete.

This (adjective) boy wants *this* toy.

Éste quiere este juguete.

This one (pronoun) wants *this* toy.

Indefinite Pronouns

Indefinite pronouns are those that do not specifically refer to anything or anyone, where the referent is indistinct. The most common are listed below.

algo something, anything
alguien someone, anyone
alguno(a)[1] some, any
nada nothing
nadie no one, nobody, not anyone
ninguno(a)[1] no one, none, not any

---

[1] Drop the **-o** before masculine singular nouns: **algún chico** *some boy.*

In a comparison (page 105) where an indefinite pronoun follows the word **que** *(than),* the negative pronoun is used, even to express the positive.

Él es más inteligente *que* nadie.	He is smarter *than anyone.*

Relative Pronouns

Relative pronouns introduce dependent clauses and can take one of several forms.

que — to express *who, whom, which, what,* and *that*
quien or **quienes** — to express *who* or *whom*
cual or **cuales** — to express *who* or *which*

Que — The most frequently used relative pronoun, **que** can refer to things as well as people, and it is used in a variety of situations.

In adjective clauses describing nouns:

La profesora *que* enseña la clase es mi vecina.	The professor *who* teaches the class is my neighbor.
El pescado *que* comió estuvo crudo.	The fish *that* she ate was raw.

With a general or unspecified subject:

***Las que* compramos volveremos sin dinero.**	*Those who* shop will return without money.

In combination with the neuter article **lo**:

Ella me dice *lo que* necesito saber.	She tells me *what* I need to know.

In object-of-preposition clauses describing things (not people):

La ciudad en *que* escribo está muriendo.	The city about *which* I write is dying.

8
prn

Quien — Quien refers to people.

In an adjective clause modifying a person:

Mi novia, *quien* es hermosa, vive en el campo.	My girlfriend, *who* is beautiful, lives in the country
El hombre *a quien* Ud. detuvo es un ladrón.	The man *whom* you stopped is a thief.
Vi *quien* entró el edificio.	I saw *who* entered the building.

In object-of-preposition clauses describing people:

Los niños con *quienes* juego salen ahora.	The children with *whom* I play are leaving now.

Cual — Cual, when used with a definite article, may be used to clarify the gender of the subject.

La novelista, *la cual* es muy popular, completó su último libro.	The novelist, *who* is very popular, completed her latest book.

9 | *A**dverbs* (adv)

To form most adverbs (generally formed in English with the *-ly* ending), the suffix **-mente** is added to the feminine form of the adjective.

profundo profound
profunda*mente* profoundly

Adverbs are also often expressed by using the word **con** *(with)* plus a noun.

rápido quick → **rápida*mente*** quickly → **con rapidez** quickly
(with speed)

If there are two or more adverbs in a series, only the last one takes on the **-mente** ending.

Ella trabajó lenta pero cuidadosa*mente*.	She worked slowly but surely.

Opposing Adverbs

abajo below	**arriba** above
algún día someday	**jamás**[1] never
algún lado somewhere	**ningún lado** nowhere
aquí here	**allí** there
bien well	**mal** badly
hoy today	**mañana** tomorrow
menos less, least	**más** more, most
peor worse, worst	**mejor** better, best
poco little	**mucho** much
siempre always	**nunca** never
también also, too	**tampoco** neither
tan so	**tanto** so much
o ... o either ... or	**ni ... ni** neither ... nor

9
adv

Double negatives are not only acceptable in Spanish but are required in sentences beginning with **no**.

No bebo *nunca.*	I never drink.

The same idea can be expressed without a double negative.

Nunca bebo.	I never drink.

---

[1] Also means *ever* in questions where a negative answer is assumed.

¿Jamás vendrás a verme?   Will you *ever* come see me?

(**Alguna vez** is used to express *ever* in other situations.)

10 | *Interrogatives* (int)

Interrogatives—the question words—always have accents, whether they come at the beginning or in the middle of a sentence.

INTERROGATIVES: THE QUESTION WORDS

how many? **¿cuántos?**	which one, what? **¿cuál?**
how much? **¿cuánto(a/os/as)?**	who, whom? **¿quién?**
how, what? **¿cómo?**	whose, of whom? **¿de quién?**
what, which? **¿qué?**	to whom? **¿a quién?**
when? **¿cuándo?**	with whom? **¿con quién?**
where to? **¿adónde?**	why (reason)? **¿por qué?**
where? **¿dónde?**	why (purpose)? **¿para qué?**

---

10 int

Qué is used when a definition, explanation, or description is sought.

> **¿*Qué* es una sardina?**　　What is a sardine?

It can also be used as an adjective, modifying the noun in question.

> **¿A *qué* hora es...?**　　At what hour is...?

Cuál is used in solicitations or when a selection is presented.

> **¿*Cuál* libro quieres?**　　Which book do you want?
> **¿*Cuál* es tu hija?**　　Which one is your daughter?

11 | *Conjunctions* (con)

Y *(and)* — This is the most common conjunction in Spanish. It functions as the word *and* in English.

el chico *y* su novia the boy *and* his girlfriend

ᕦᐟ **Note**

> **Y** changes to **e** before **i-** and **hi-** but not before **hie-**.
>
> **ahorrar e invertir** to save and invest
> **acero y hierro** steel and iron

Pero *(but)* — **Pero** is used to express *yet* and *however*.

Fui a la fiesta, *pero* no   I went to the party, *but* no one
había nadie.   was there.

Sino *(but)* — **Sino** is used to express *but rather* and *except*.

No tengo nada *sino* esto.   I have nothing *but* this.

When the second clause is independent, **sino** is often used in combination with **que**.

No fui a la fiesta *sino que*   I did not go to the party *but*
me quedé en casa.   stayed in the house.

O *(or)* — The word **o** represents the Spanish word for *or* and *either*.

hombre *o* ratón man *or* mouse
***o* martes *o* jueves** *either* Tuesday *or* Thursday

The **o** changes to **u** before words beginning with **o-** and **ho-**.

lago *u* océano lake *or* ocean

Ni *(nor)* — The word **ni** represents the Spanish word for *nor* and *neither*.

ni **pescado** *ni* **ave**	*neither* fish *nor* fowl

For identification of relational conjunctions, see page 62.

COMMON CONJUNCTIONS

antes (de) **que** before	**ni siquiera** not even
así que as soon as, after	**o** or, either
aun even, still	**para que** in order that, so that
aunque although, even though, even if	**pero** but, yet
como as, since, how	**porque** because
como si as if	**puesto que** although, since, as long as
con tal (de) **que** provided that	**que** that, because
cuando when	**si** if, whether
después (de) **que** after	**sin embargo** nevertheless, however
en cuanto as soon as	**sino** but, but rather
hasta que until	**y** and
mientras while, as long as	
ni nor, neither	

---

12 | *Prepositions* (pre)

The Preposition *A*

The preposition **a** is used extensively in Spanish. In many cases the **a** is not translatable into English, as a direct translation would be awkward, redundant, or unnecessary. The following are some of the cases where **a** is used.

Specific place or point in time:

a **las siete y media**	at 7:30
Está *a* **la puerta.**	She is at the door.

Price:

a **diez dólares...**	for $10.00...

Method:

Lo hizo *a* mano.	He did it by hand.

Destination:

Fue *a* la playa.	She went to the beach.
Vamos *a* Italia.	We're going to Italy.

Invitation or exhortation:

Nos invitó *a* una fiesta.	He invited us to a party.

Indirect object (page 37):

Dáselo *a* Carlos.	Give it to Carlos.

Between two verbs:

Voy *a* cantar.	I am going to sing.
Empezó *a* nevar.	It began to snow.

The preposition **a** is also used after a verb when the direct object is

1. a person:

    Conozco *a* su esposa.   I know your wife.

2. an indefinite personal pronoun:

    No veo *a* nadie.   I don't see anyone.

3. a domesticated animal:

    Busco *a* mi perro.   I am looking for my dog.

4. a geographic location in the position of a direct object:

    Queremos visitar *a* Perú.   We want to visit Peru.

5. a personified noun:

Teme *a* la muerte.   He fears death

COMMON VERBS REQUIRING THE PREPOSITION *A*

ayudar to help	**invitar** to invite
buscar to look for	**llamar** to call
cuidar to care for	**mirar** to look at
esperar to wait for	**visitar** to visit

The preposition **a** is not used in the following cases.

With impersonal nouns or pronouns:

Busco mis zapatos.   I am looking for my shoes.

With collective nouns:

Anoche oímos el grupo musical.   Last night we heard the musical group.

After forms of the verb **tener** *(to have)*:

Teníamos tres gallinas.   We had three chickens.

The Preposition *De*

The preposition ***de*** is used to indicate

possession:

la casa *del* hombre the man's house
la casa *de* Juan Juan's house

origin:

Soy *de* Texas.   I'm from Texas.

cause:

> **El hombre sufre *de* cáncer.**   The man suffers from cancer.

part of day:

> **a las dos *de* la tarde**   at 2:00 in the afternoon

material:

> **la casa *de* ladrillo**   brick house

color (with the word *color*):

> ***de* color blanco, verde, etc.**   of the color white, green, etc.

condition or attribute:

> **la mujer *de* la boca grande**   the woman with the big mouth

function:

> **La música es *de* relajar.**   The music is for relaxing.

and with another preposition followed by an infinitive:

> **después *de* bailar**   After dancing

The Prepositions *Para* and *Por*

Para expresses destination, limitation, and reason. Here are some of the cases where **para** is used.

Movement toward a specific destination:

> **Salgo ahora *para* la escuela.**   I'm leaving *for* school now.

Something for someone's benefit:

> **El coche es *para* Raúl.**   The car is *for* Raul.

Purpose or function:

Estudia *para* aprender.	He studies *in order to* learn.
Es una caja *para* joyas.	It's a box *for* jewels.

Deadline, time limit, or future time:

***Para* el jueves, estaré in Francia.**	*By* Thursday, I will be in France.

To be ready to or *to be about to* (with **estar** and an infinitive):

Están *para* venir ahora.	They are ready *to* come now.

End or future plan:

Ella estudia *para* llegar a ser abogada.	She studies to be a lawyer.

Incongruous description:

Es muy alto *para* su edad.	He is tall *for* his age.

12 pre

Por is even more common than **para**. Here are some situations described with **por**.

Movement without limits:

Pasamos *por* varios pueblos.	We passed *through* several towns.
Caminamos *por* la orilla.	We walk *by* the shore.

Substitution:

Lavé el perro *por* María.	I washed the dog in Maria's place.

Exchange for:

¿Cuánto pagaste *por* el pan?	How much did you pay *for* the bread?

Approximate location (in space and time):

Aquí reparan los carros *por* **la noche.**	Cars are fixed here *at* night.
Mi coche está *por* **aquí.**	My car is around here.

Modes of transportation:

Mis hermanos viajan *por* **tren**.	My brothers travel *by* train.

Number or measure:

Lo hacen *por* **libra.**	They make it *by* the pound.

Specific reason or objective:

Alfredo fue al super-mercado *por* **la leche.**	Alfred went to the supermarket *for* some milk.

And with infinitives to indicate what is left to be done:

Quedan muchas pá-ginas *por* **leer.**	There remain many pages *to* read.

**12
pre**

OTHER COMMON PREPOSITIONS

a to, at, in, on, by	**después (de)** afterward
a causa (de) because of	**detrás (de)** behind
a pesar (de) in spite of	**durante** during
acerca (de) about, concerning	**en** in, on, by
además (de) besides	**encima (de)** over, above
al lado (de) beside	**entre** between
alrededor (de) about, around	**frente (a)** opposite to
antes (de) before, sooner	**hacia** toward, about
atrás behind	**hasta** until, even
bajo under	**junto (a)** next to
con with	**salvo** except
contra against	**según** according to
debajo (de) under, below	**sin (que)** without
delante (de) in front of	**sobre** over, about
dentro (de) inside, within	**(a) través (de)** through
desde from, since	

13 | Summary of Pronouns (spr)

13
spr

SUBJECT PRONOUNS (PAGE 32)

1st Person	**yo** I	**nosotros(as)** we
2nd Person *(fam.)*	**tú** you	**vosotros(as)** you
3rd Person, 2nd *(form.)*	**él, ella, usted** he/she/you	**ellos(as), ustedes** they/you

---

PREPOSITIONAL PRONOUNS (PAGE 33)

1st Person	**mí** me	**nosotros(as)** us
2nd Person *(fam.)*	**ti** you	**vosotros(as)** you
3rd Person, 2nd *(form.)*	**él, ella, usted** him/her/you	**ellos(as), ustedes** them/you

---

POSSESSIVE (ADJECTIVE) PRONOUNS (PAGE 34)

Before noun:

1st Person	**mi(s)** my	**nuestro(a/os/as)** our
2nd Person *(fam.)*	**tu(s)** your	**vuestro(a/os/as)** your
3rd Person, 2nd *(form.)*	**su(s)** his/her/your	**su(s)** their, your

(continued)

After noun or alone:		
1st Person	**mío(a/os/as)** mine	**nuestro(a/os/as)** ours
2nd Person *(fam.)*	**tuyo(a/os/as)** yours	**vuestro(a/os/as)** yours
3rd Person, 2nd *(form.)*	**suyo(a/os/as)** his/hers/yours	**suyo(a/os/as)** theirs/yours

REFLEXIVE PRONOUNS (PAGE 35)

1st Person	**me** myself	**nos** ourselves
2nd Person *(fam.)*	**te** yourself	**os** yourselves
3rd Person, 2nd *(form.)*	**se** himself/herself/yourself	**se** themselves, yourselves

DIRECT OBJECT PRONOUNS (PAGE 36)

1st Person	**me** me	**nos** us
2nd Person *(fam.)*	**te** you	**os** you
3rd Person, 2nd *(form.)*	**lo, le** him/you (m.)/it **la** her/you (f.)/it	**los (las)** them/you

INDIRECT OBJECT PRONOUNS (PAGE 37)

1st Person	**me** me	**nos** us
2nd Person *(fam.)*	**te** you	**os** you
3rd Person, 2nd *(form.)*	**le** him/her/you/it	**les** them/you

13
spr

DEMONSTRATIVE PRONOUNS (PAGE 40)

	Masculine	*Feminine*	*Neuter*
this	**éste**	**ésta**	**esto**
these	**éstos**	**éstas**	**estos**
that	**ése**	**ésa**	**eso**
those	**ésos**	**ésas**	**esos**
that (distant)	**aquél**	**aquélla**	**aquello**
those (distant)	**aquéllos**	**aquéllas**	**aquellos**

RELATIVE PRONOUNS (PAGE 41)

que who, whom, which, what, that
quien(es) who, whom
cual(es) who, which

14 | V*erb* O*verview* (ovw)

Spanish verbs are referred to in their infinitive form, which is one word ending in **-ar**, **-er**, or **-ir**.

> **conquistar** to conquer **ver** to see **venir** to come

Spanish verbs are considerably more varied than English verbs because, when conjugated, they not only indicate tense, but also person (subject) and number.

For example, verb forms in English in the present tense of the verb *to walk* vary only in the 3rd person singular, with the addition of *-s*.

I walk	we walk
you walk	you (plural) walk
he, she, it walk*s*	they walk

In Spanish, however, verb forms change according to the subject and number.

yo camino	**nosotros camin*amos***
tú camin*as*	**vosotros camin*áis***
él, **ella**, **usted camin*a***	**ellos(as)**, **ustedes camin*an***

Because of this property, Spanish verbs often stand on their own, *without* a *subject pronoun*:

Camino.	*I walk.*
Yo camino.	*I walk.*

Most verb forms are created by dropping the **-ar**, **-er**, or **-ir** from the infinitive (leaving the infinitive stem) and adding other endings, although the future tense and the conditional tense are created by *adding on* to the infinitive.

Note that in most cases, treatment of **-er** and **-ir** verbs, in terms of changing verb endings, is generally the same. Accordingly, they are paired together.

Verbs following the general formation rules are called regular verbs. **Hablar,** for example, the verb infinitive *to speak,* follows the general pattern in all tenses, so it is considered a regular *-ar* verb. Fortunately for the student of Spanish, most verbs are regular; and, even irregular verbs follow patterns. Unfortunately most common verbs are usually irregular. In these cases, the different verb forms simply have to be memorized. To assist in this process, full conjugations of thirty common verbs are presented in Appendix C. At first, learning the various verb forms seems an overwhelming task; but the following overview should help.

There are five simple, or one-word, tenses.

1. The *present tense* (page 58) works much like the present tense in English. It expresses things that are happening now or that happen normally.

    Yo *hablo* español.   I *speak* Spanish.

2. The *preterite tense* (page 64) expresses something begun or completed at a specific time in the past.

    ***Corté* el césped ayer.**   Yesterday I *mowed* the grass.

3. The *imperfect tense* (page 65) expresses something that was *in progress* in the past.

    ***Cortaba* el césped   I *was cutting* the grass when...
    cuando...**

4. The *future tense* (page 69) expresses things yet to happen.

    ***Comeré* más tarde.**   I *will eat* later.

5. The *conditional tense* (page 70) suggests what would happen.

    **Me *gustaría* visitar   I *would like* to visit Spain.
    España.**

Beyond this straightforward base, verbs become more complicated. There are two moods (the indicative and the subjunctive) in both the present and imperfect tenses. Additionally, there are present and past participles, seven compound tenses, various command

**14
ovw**

forms...and so on. The treatment of verbs that follows, however, is intended to present the information succinctly and to point out helpful patterns along the way.

15 | *Present* *Tenses* (prt)

Present Indicative

The present indicative is used to describe an actual situation in the current time, and it is formed by dropping the **-ar**, **-er**, or **-ir** from the infinitive and adding the endings listed here.

	-ar Verbs		**-er**, **-ir** Verbs	
1st Person	**-o**	**-amos**	**-o**	**-emos, -imos**
2nd Person *(fam.)*	**-as**	-áis	**-es**	-éis, -ís
3rd Person, 2nd *(form.)*	**-a**	**-an**	**-e**	**-en**

The present indicative tense is used to describe events occurring now or events that occur regularly.

Juan *estudia* en la biblioteca. { Juan *is studying* in the library.
Juan *studies* in the library.

It can be used to express a near future condition.

***Salgo* para España la semana que viene.** I *am leaving* for Spain next week.

It may also express *past* tense in narrations relating historical events.

Colón *descubre* el nuevo mundo en 1492. Columbus *discovers* the new world in 1492.

```
         SOME IRREGULAR VERBS IN THE
            PRESENT INDICATIVE

    (only the first person - yo - forms are irregular)

  caer  fall        →   caigo     saber  know    →   sé
  dar  give         →   doy       salir  leave   →   salgo
  hacer  do, make   →   hago      traer  bring   →   traigo
  poner  put        →   pongo     valer  value   →   valgo

  Also see the 30 common verbs beginning on page 153.
```

Present Progressive

The present progressive tense is used to express what is happening at the moment. It is expressed by combining the present tense form of the verb **estar** and the present participle of the action verb. To see how the present participle is formed, turn to page 81.

Form of **estar** *(to be)* + *Present Participle*

***Estoy hablando* por teléfono.**	I *am speaking* on the phone.
***Está comiendo* con su amigo.**	She *is eating* with her friend.
***Están viviendo* en California.**	They *are living* in California.

15
prt

Present Subjunctive

While the present indicative mood is used to describe an actual situation, the present subjunctive mood expresses uncertainty, feelings, desires, and hypothetical situations.

To form the subjunctive, drop the **-o** from the first person singular form of the present indicative and add the endings at the top of the next page. All but six verbs — **dar, estar, haber, ir, saber**, and **ser** — follow this pattern. See page 63.

In the subjunctive, **-ar** verbs take **-e** and **-er/-ir** verbs take **-a.**

PRESENT SUBJUNCTIVE		
	-ar Verbs	**-er, -ir** Verbs
1st Person	**-e** **-emos**	**-a** **-amos**
2nd Person *(fam.)*	**-es** -éis	**-as** -áis
3rd Person, 2nd *(form.)*	**-e** **-en**	**-a** **-an**

Iré al cine cuando tenga dinero.	I will go to the movies *when I have money.*

When to Use the Subjunctive

The subjunctive mood is called for when the situation is not factual, but rather when the action is subjective or hypothetical. In Spanish, the speaker simply needs to recognize when the action is real and objective (indicative) — *He brings me a towel.* — and when it is subjective (subjunctive) — *I hope that he brings me a towel.* — and use appropriate verb endings. The subjunctive can be expressed in the present and in the past. There are also present perfect and past perfect forms.

A helpful way to recognize situations calling for the hypothetical subjunctive is to ask yourself the the following questions:

1. Is there a possibility that this action has not occurred or is not now occurring?
2. Is the action or event contained in a dependent clause?

If the answer to both questions is yes, the subjunctive mood should be used.

In Spanish, as in English, there are three grammatical moods: the imperative, the indicative, and the subjunctive. In English, very few structural changes are employed to signify a change in mood. In Spanish, however, mood changes necessitate different verb endings. Correctly using the subjunctive mood is one of the most non-intuitive aspects of Spanish for English-speaking students; but it is not that complicated!

15 prt

The subjunctive is used

1. in expressions of preference, desire, and hope:

    When the verb in the independent clause is a verb such as **desear** *to desire,* **querer** *to want,* **esperar** *to hope,* and **preferir** *to prefer,* the dependent clause uses the subjunctive.

    Prefiero que no *veas*   I prefer that you not watch
    ese programa.   that show.

    Quiero que ustedes   I want you to behave well.
    se *porten* bien.

2. in expressions of permission, request, advice, suggestion, command, and prohibition:

aconsejar to advise	**pedir** to ask for
decir to tell	**permitir**[1] to permit
dejar to let	**prohibir**[1] to forbid
escribir to write	**rogar** to beg
exigir to demand	**recomendar** to recommend
insistir to insist	**sugerir** to suggest
mandar[1] to order	**suplicar** to beg

    Me aconsejaron que   They advised me to leave.
    saliera.

3. in expressions of fear, joy, surprise, regret, and sorrow:

    alegrar(se) to be happy
    sorprender(se) to surprise
    sentir to regret
    temer to fear

    Temo que no *vuelva a*   I am afraid he won't return on
    tiempo.   time.

    Se alegra que yo *vaya*   He is happy that I am going to
    a la fiesta.   the party.

    **15
    prt**

---

[1] These verbs may be followed by other verbs in the subjunctive *or* the infinitive.

4. in expressions of denial, doubt, and disbelief:

no creer to disbelieve
dudar to doubt
negar to deny

No creen que yo *llame* más tarde.	They don't believe I'll call later.
Negamos que *sea* la verdad.	We deny that it is the truth.

5. after indication of *perhaps:*

acaso   quizás   tal vez

Acaso *visite* este otoño.   Perhaps she is visiting this fall.

6. after the following expressions, provided that doubt, uncertainty, or emotion is suggested or implied:

Es bueno It is good
Es difícil It is hard
Es dudoso It is doubtful
Es importante It is important
Es imposible It is impossible
Es incierto It is uncertain
Es malo It is bad
Es mejor It is better
Es necesario It is necessary
Es posible It is possible
Es una lástima It is a pity

7. after the following conjunctions, if doubt or anticipation is implied:

a menos que unless
a pesar de que in spite of
antes (de) que before
aunque although
cuando when

15
prt

después (de) **que** after

en caso (de) **que** in case

en cuanto as soon as

hasta que until

para que so that

8. in formal commands. See page 76.

ONLY SIX IRREGULAR VERBS IN THE PRESENT SUBJUNCTIVE

	dar *to give*		**estar** *to be*	
1st Person	**dé**	**demos**	**esté**	**estemos**
2nd Person *(fam.)*	**des**	deis	**estés**	estéis
3rd Person, 2nd *(form.)*	**dé**	**den**	**esté**	**estén**

	haber *to have* (auxiliary)		**ir** *to go*	
1st Person	**haya**	**hayamos**	vaya	**vayamos**
2nd Person *(fam.)*	**hayas**	hayáis	**vayas**	vayáis
3rd Person, 2nd *(form.)*	**haya**	**hayan**	vaya	**vayan**

	saber *to know*		**ser** *to be*	
1st Person	**sepa**	**sepamos**	sea	**seamos**
2nd Person *(fam.)*	**sepas**	sepáis	**seas**	seáis
3rd Person, 2nd *(form.)*	**sepa**	**sepan**	sea	**sean**

**15
prt**

16 | *P*ast *T*enses (pat)

The Preterite Tense

The preterite is used to describe actions completed in the past.

PRETERITE TENSE				
	-ar Verbs		**-er, -ir** Verbs	
1st Person	**-é**	**-amos**	**-í**	**-imos**
2nd Person *(fam.)*	**-aste**	-asteis	**-iste**	-isteis
3rd Person, 2nd *(form.)*	**-ó**	**-aron**	**-ió**	**-ieron**

Yo *terminé* mi tarea anoche.

I *finished* my homework last night.

The preterite tense is used to describe past actions completed at a specific time or in a specific number of times. It is formed by dropping the **-ar**, **-er**, or **-ir** from the infinitive and adding the endings listed above.

16 pat

SOME IRREGULAR VERBS IN THE PRETERITE TENSE		
dar to give	**di**	**dimos**
	diste	disteis
	dio	**dieron**
ver to see	**vi**	**vimos**
	viste	visteis
	vio	**vieron**

In the preterite tense, **ir** *(to go)* and **ser** *(to be)* have the same form.

fui	**fuimos**
fuiste	fuisteis
fue	**fueron**

Change to **u** in stem:

andar	to walk	**(anduve)**
estar	to be	**(estuve)**
poder	to be able to	**(pude)**
poner	to put	**(puse)**
saber	to know	**(supe)**
tener	to have	**(tuve)**

Change to **i** in stem:

hacer	to do, to make	**(hice)**
querer	to want	**(quise)**
venir	to come	**(vine)**

Change to **j** in stem:

decir	to tell	**(dije)**
producir	to produce	**(produje)**
traer	to bring	**(traje)**

Imperfect Indicative Tense

The imperfect indicative tense is used to describe continuing or repeated actions in the past. It is formed by dropping the **-ar**, **-er**, or **-ir** from the infinitive and adding the endings listed below.

IMPERFECT INDICATIVE TENSE				
	-ar Verbs		**-er, -ir** Verbs	
1st Person	**-aba**	**-ábamos**	**-ía**	**-íamos**
2nd Person *(fam.)*	**-abas**	-abais	**-ías**	-íais
3rd Person, 2nd *(form.)*	**-aba**	**-aban**	**-ía**	**-ían**

16
pat

Juanita *estudiaba* en su cuarto.	{	Juanita *was studying* in her room. Juanita *studied* in her room.

The imperfect indicative tense is also used if the meaning suggests *used to:*

Yo *esquiaba* todos los inviernos.	I *used to ski* every winter.

when describing states or conditions in the past:

Estaban contentos.	They *were* content.
Ella *tenía* los ojos azules.	She *had* blue eyes.

to tell time in the past:

Eran las once.	It *was* eleven.

There are only three irregular verbs in the imperfect tense.

ir *to go*		**ser** *to be*		**ver** *to see*	
iba	**íbamos**	**era**	**éramos**	**veía**	**veíamos**
ibas	ibais	**eras**	erais	**veías**	veías
iba	**iban**	**era**	**eran**	**veía**	**veían**

Some verbs have different meanings in the preterite and the imperfect tenses. (Note that examples shown are in the first person singular.)

	Preterite		Imperfect	
conocer	**conocí**	I met	**conocía**	I knew (was familiar with)
saber	**supe**	I found out	**sabía**	I knew (a fact)
querer	**quise**	I tried to	**quería**	I wanted to
no querer	**no quise**	I refused to	**no quería**	I did not want to
poder	**pude**	I managed to	**podía**	I was capable of
no poder	**no pude**	I failed to	**no podía**	I was not capable of
tener	**tuve**	I received	**tenía**	I possessed

16
pat

The Imperfect Subjunctive

The imperfect or past subjunctive is used in situations where the verb in the independent clause is in the past or conditional tense. This tense is used to express something that might have been or would have been.

IMPERFECT SUBJUNCTIVE					
1st Person	**-ra**	**-ramos**[1]		**-se**	**-semos**
2nd Person *(fam.)*	**-ras**	-rais	OR	**-ses**	-seis
3rd Person, 2nd *(form.)*	**-ra**	**-ran**		**-se**	**-sen**

Dudaba que él *matara*   I doubted that he *killed* the cat.
el gato.

The imperfect subjunctive tense is formed by:

1. taking the verb's third person plural form of the preterite tense (page 64),
2. dropping the **-ron** from the end, and
3. adding the endings above.

There are no irregularities in the imperfect subjunctive tense because any irregularities in conjugation will already be reflected in the third person plural preterite form.

Either set of endings may be used to form the imperfect subjunctive. The set on the left is more common. The endings are the same for **-ar, -er** and **-ir** verbs.

The imperfect subjunctive expresses the same situations as the present subjunctive in the past. See page 61.

---

[1] with an accent on the **a** or **e** in the root component: (**comiéramos**, we might have eaten).

The imperfect subjunctive may also be used to express the conditional tense with the verbs **querer** *(to want)* and **poder** *(to be able to)*.

Quisiera... I would like...
Pudiéramos... We would be able to...

The Imperfect Progressive

The imperfect or past progressive can be used to stress what was happening in the past. The imperfect progressive is expressed by combining the correct imperfect form of the verb **estar** and the present participle of the action verb. To see how the present participle is formed, turn to page 81.

Imperfect of **estar** *(to be)* + *Present Participle*

estaba	estábamos
estabas	estabais
estaba	estaban

Estaba montando.   I *was riding.*

Recent Past Condition

**16
pat**

The recent past condition is used to describe something that just happened. It is expressed by combining a present or imperfect form of the verb **acabar** with the preposition **de** and the infinitive of the action verb.

Form of **acabar** *(to complete)* + **de** + *Infinitive*

Acabo de terminar mis estudios.   I *have just finished* my studies.

Acababa de comer cuando llegó Pedro con una pizza.   I *had just eaten* when Pedro arrived with a pizza.

17 | *F*uture and *C*onditional *T*enses (fct)

The Future Tense

The future tense describes events in the future.

The future tense is formed by adding the following endings to the infinitive. The same endings are used for **-ar**, **-er**, and **-ir** verbs.

FUTURE TENSE		
1st Person	**-é**	**-emos**
2nd Person *(fam.)*	**-ás**	-éis
3rd Person, 2nd *(form.)*	**-á**	**-án**

Yo *iré* a Europa el año que viene.	I *will go* to Europe next year.

The future tense is also used to express uncertainty or speculation in the present.

***Estará* en el camino.**	He *is probably* on the road.

Near Future Condition

The near future condition expresses something about to happen. The English equivalent is "going to." The near future is expressed by combining a form of the verb **ir** with the preposition **a** and the infinitive of the action verb.

17 fct

Form of **ir** *(to go)* + **a** + *Infinitive*

Voy a comer.	I am going to eat.
Vamos a hablar.	We are going to speak.

An invitation or suggestion can be expressed with the near future condition, using the first person plural form of the construction.

Vamos a tomar un café.   *Let's have* coffee.

Note that the present subjunctive is another way to express a suggestion, command, or an invitation (page 78), and in fact must be used if the suggestion is negative.

No *vayamos* a tomar   *Let's not have* coffee today.
café hoy.

SER AND ESTAR IN THE FUTURE AND CONDITIONAL TENSES

Future		Conditional	
ser	**seré** **seremos**	**sería**	**seríamos**
	serás seréis	**serías**	seríais
	será **serán**	**sería**	**serían**
estar	**estaré** **estaremos**	**estaría**	**estaríamos**
	estarás estaréis	**estarías**	estaríais
	estará **estarán**	**estaría**	**estarían**

The Conditional Tense

The conditional expresses what would happen.

It is formed by adding the following endings to the infinitive. The same endings are used for **-ar**, **-er**, and **-ir** verbs.

THE CONDITIONAL TENSE		
1st Person	**-ía**	**-íamos**
2nd Person *(fam.)*	**-ías**	-íais
3rd Person, 2nd *(form.)*	**-ía**	**-ían**

Iría **allí.**	I *would go* there.
¿Podría **prestármelo?**	*Would* you lend it to me?

The conditional tense is used

to express *would* regarding future events:

Me *gustaría* visitarlo.	I *would like* to visit him.

to express uncertainty in the past:

Estaría **allí todo el tiempo.**	It *was probably* there the whole time.

to express a polite statement or request:

¿Podría **pasarme la sal?**	*Would you* pass me the salt?

There are a few irregular forms of the future and conditional tenses. The following are some common examples, using the first person singular for illustration purposes.

17
fct

	Future	Conditional
All drop the **a, e,** or **i.**		
caber (to fit) →	**cabré** →	**cabría**
haber (to have) →	**habré** →	**habría**
poder (to be able) →	**podré** →	**podría**
querer (to want) →	**querré** →	**querría**
saber (to know) →	**sabré** →	**sabría**
		(continued)

	Future	*Conditional*
Some drop the **c**		
decir (to tell) →	**diré** →	**diría**
hacer (to make) →	**haré** →	**haría**
Or add a **d**		
poner (to put) →	**pondré** →	**pondría**
salir (to leave) →	**saldré** →	**saldría**
tener (to have) →	**tendré** →	**tendría**
valer (to be worth) →	**valdré** →	**valdría**
venir (to come) →	**vendré** →	**vendría**

18 | *Perfect Tenses* (pet)

18 pet

A compound tense is one made up of two or more words, and certain examples of compound tense appear elsewhere, such as in the present progressive tense, when a form of the verb **estar** (*to be*) is combined with the present participle of another verb. (See page 59.)

A perfect tense, in Spanish and in English, is a type of compound tense that is made up of a form of an auxiliary verb—**haber** *to have*—in combination with the past participle of another verb. (See page 82 for a description of the past participle.) Not only are the perfect tenses formed similarly in the two languages, but they also function similarly.

Carlos *ha regado*   Carlos *has watered* the garden.
el jardín.

In Spanish, there are four commonly used perfect tenses, which are described below. In addition, both the present perfect and the past perfect tenses have forms for both the indicative and subjunctive moods. (Conditions calling for use of the subjunctive are described on page 61.)

The verb **haber** is an auxiliary verb which translates to English as *to have*. The verb **tener** is used to mean *to have* as in *to possess*.

1. *Present Perfect Tense* — The present perfect tense is used to express an action or event in the past without reference to a specific time or duration. Often it is used to describe a recent or continuing event in the past. It is formed with **haber** in the present tense plus the past participle.

   Ella *ha ido* a la tienda.   She *has gone* to the store.

   Remember that the meanings *have just* and *had just* are expressed with the verb **acabar** (page 68).

2. *Past Perfect (or Pluperfect) Tense* — The past perfect tense is used to express a past action or event that is completed before another past action or event. It is formed with **haber** in the imperfect tense plus the past participle.

   ized *Habían llegado* **muchas**   They *had arrived* many
   horas antes del sol.   hours before the sun.

   Note that there is also a preterite perfect tense—sometimes referred to as the past anterior—which is occasionally used in combination with a time expression, such as **cuando** (when) or **después que** (after which), to indicate something that had been completed immediately before another past action. In this case, the preterite form of **haber** (page 164) is used with the past participle.

3. *Future Perfect Tense* — The future perfect tense is used to express a future action or event that will have been completed before another future action or event. It is formed with **haber** in the future tense plus the past participle.

   Después de este niño,   After this child, the woman *will*
   la mujer *habrá parido*   *have given birth* six times.
   seis veces.

4. *Conditional Perfect Tense* — The conditional perfect tense is used to express a contrary-to-fact action or event in the past— one that *would have* occurred if something else had not happened. It is formed with **haber** in the conditional tense plus the past participle.

Los chicos se _habrían detenido_ si hubieran sabido que no es correcto.	The boys _would have stopped_ if they had known it was wrong.

The future perfect and conditional perfect tenses are also used to express probability.

Ella _habrá parido_ muchas veces.	She _must have given birth_ many times.
Ella _habría parido_ muchas veces.	She _had probably given birth_ many times.

The full conjugation of **haber** is shown on page 164. The forms of **haber** as they are used in the common perfect tenses are summarized in the table below.

The form **haber** and the past participle should not be separated by any other word or words. For example, negation is always accomplished by using **no** before the conjugated form of **haber**. Reflexive pronouns should also go before the conjugated form of **haber**.

18 pet

SUMMARY OF THE PERFECT TENSES

Present Perfect — has, have

he	hemos		**ha escogido**
has	habéis	+ _Past Participle_	he has chosen
ha	**han**		

Present Perfect Subjunctive — may have

haya	**hayamos**		**hayamos pensado**
hayas	hayáis	+ _Past Participle_	we may have
haya	**hayan**		thought

Past Perfect — had

había	**habíamos**		**habían creído**
habías	habíais	+ _Past Participle_	they had believed
había	**habían**		

(continued)

Past Perfect Subjunctive — might have

hubiera	**hubiéramos**		**hubiera llovido**
hubieras	hubierais	+ *Past Participle*	it might have
hubiera	**hubieran**		rained

Future Perfect — will have

habré	**habremos**		**habrá comido** he
habrás	habréis	+ *Past Participle*	will have eaten
habrá	**habrán**		

Conditional Perfect — would have

habría	**habríamos**		**habría venido** I
habrías	habríais	+ *Past Participle*	would have come
habría	**habrían**		

Perfect Participles

Present	**habiendo**	+ *Past Participle*	**habiendo visto**
			having seen
Past	**habido**		**Ha habido...**
			There has/have
			been...

18
pet

19 | *C*ommands (com)

Commands may be issued directly or by way of suggestion. The several command forms used in Spanish are described here.

Formal Direct Commands

Formal direct commands are formed by adding the **usted** and **ustedes** endings of the present subjunctive to the **yo** form of the present indicative after dropping the **-o.**

> **comer** (to eat) → **Como.** (I eat.) → **Coma.** (Eat.)

Com*a* cereal en la mañana.	*Eat* cereal in the morning.
No bail*en* más de dos horas.	*Don't dance* more than two hours.

Irregularities and stem changes in the **yo** form of the present tense usually remain in the command form.

***Duerma* por lo menos ocho horas.**	*Sleep* at least eight hours.

If an object pronoun is involved, it attaches to an affirmative command,

Díga*me* la verdad.	Tell *me* the truth.

and precedes a negative one.

No *me* diga que usted no lo sabe.	Don't tell *me* that you don't know.

If a direct and indirect object pronoun are used, they attach to the affirmative command, with the indirect object pronoun going before the direct object pronoun, and an accent is added to the command.

Dé*me*lo.	Give it (masculine) to *me*.

Dé*se***lo**.	Give it (masculine) to *him/her*
	you / them.
Dé*nos***lo**.	Give it (masculine) to *us.*

The following are some formal direct commands that are irregular:

dar	to give	→	**dé**
decir	to tell	→	**diga**
estar	to be	→	**esté**
hacer	to do, make	→	**haga**
ir	to go	→	**vaya**
oír	to hear	→	**oiga**
poner	to put	→	**ponga**
saber	to know	→	**sepa**
ser	to be	→	**sea**
tener	to have	→	**tenga**
traer	to bring	→	**traiga**
venir	to come	→	**venga**
ver	to see	→	**vea**

FORMAL COMMANDS OF DIRECTION

stop **pare(n)**	follow me **síga(n)me**
continue **siga(n)**	go up **suba(n)**
pass **pase(n)**	go down **baje(n)**
take **tome(n)**	get in/on (bus, etc.) **súba(n)se a**
turn **doble(n)**	get off (bus, etc.) **báje(n)se de**

19
com

Familiar Direct Commands (the *tú* form)

Informal commands are formed with the **tú** form of the present tense.

Affirmative Commands: Drop **-s** from the 2nd person singular form of the present indicative.

mirar (to look)   →   **Miras.** (You look.)   →   **Mira.** (Look.)

Negative Commands: Use 2nd person singular form of the present subjunctive.

No mires. (Don't look.)

The following are some common irregular familiar **tú** commands in the affirmative and the negative.

		Affirmative	*Negative*
decir to tell	→	**di**	**no digas**
hacer to do, make	→	**haz**	**no hagas**
ir to go	→	**ve**	**no vayas**
poner to put	→	**pon**	**no pongas**
salir to leave	→	**sal**	**no salgas**
ser to be	→	**sé**	**no seas**
tener to have	→	**ten**	**no tengas**
valer to value	→	**val**	**no valgas**
venir to come	→	**ven**	**no vengas**

Suggestion Commands

The first person plural of the present subjunctive is used in suggestion (or "Let's") commands.

Trabaj*emos* ahora.	Let's work now.
Le*amos*.	Let's read.
Tom*emos* un refresco.	Let's have a drink.

Pronouns attach to affirmative suggestion commands and precede negative ones.

Invitémos*lo*.	Let's invite him.
No *lo* invitemos.	Let's not invite him.

Soft Commands

Soft commands are used in situations where a certain action is expected or desired. This type of command is formed with an imper-

**19
com**

sonal verb phrase in the first clause and the subjunctive mood in the second clause.

Quiero que usted ...   I want you to (that you)...
vuelva pronto.   return soon.

Common examples of impersonal verb phrases used in soft commands include:

to want that...	**querer que...**
to suggest that...	**sugerir que...**
to prefer that...	**preferir que...**
to need that...	**necesitar que...**
to wish that...	**esperar que...**
I wish that...	**Ojalá que...**
to advise that...	**aconsejar que...**
to recommend that...	**recomendar que...**
to pray that...	**rezar que...**
It's necessary that...	**Es necesario que...**
It's preferable that...	**Es preferible que...**
It's (very) important that...	**Es (muy) importante que...**
It's better that...	**Es mejor que...**

Pronouns precede the conjugated verb in the dependent clause of a soft command:

Necesito que usted *me*   I need you to bring *it to me.*
***lo* traiga.**

19
com

Indirect Commands

Indirect commands are formed by omitting the initial word or words of the impersonal verb phrase in the soft command.

Quiero que manejen.   →   **¡Que manejen!**
I want them to drive.   Have them drive!

Quiero que lo termine.   →   **¡Que lo termine!**
I want him to finish.   Let him finish!

20 | *More on Verbs (mrv)*

Reflexive Verbs

Reflexive verbs describe actions done *and* received by the subject. The rules of conjugation for reflexive verbs are no different. The only difference in their conjugation is the use of reflexive pronouns. (See page 35.) The reflexive pronouns precede conjugated verbs and follow, attached to, commands and verbs in the infinitive.

Me **voy.**	I am leaving.
Me **pongo la ropa.**	I put on my clothes.
¡Báña*te*!	Bathe youself.

When a reflexive verb refers to the human body, the direct object is preceded by a definite article and not a possessive pronoun:

Necesito lavarme *las* manos.	I need to wash my hands.
Me duele *la* cabeza.	My head hurts.

SOME COMMON REFLEXIVE VERBS

aburrir(se) to get bored	**enojar**(se) to get mad
acostar(se) to lie down	**equivocar**(se) to make
afeitar(se) to shave	a mistake
bañar(se) to bathe	**ir**(se) to go away
caer(se) to fall down	**lavar**(se) to wash
callar(se) to be quiet	**levantar**(se) to get up
cansar(se) to get tired	**peinar**(se) to comb
cepillar(se) to brush	**poner**(se) to put on
despedir(se) to say goodbye	**preparar**(se) to get ready
despertar(se) to wake up	**quitar**(se) to take off
divertir(se) to have fun	**sentir**(se) to feel

The Passive Voice

The passive voice is used when the subject is the recipient of the action. It is often expressed with a form of the verb **ser** followed by the past participle of the main verb. Since the past participle is used as an adjective, it must agree in gender and number with the subject.

Form of **ser** *(to be)* + *Past Participle*

Soy amada por Juan.	*I am loved* by Juan.
El libro fue escrito	The book *was written*
por el profesor.	by the professor.
La casa ha sido construi-	The house *has been built*
da por mi padre.	by my father.

Note that this construction is often followed by **por.**

The word **se** is also used to convey the passive voice.

Se darán regalos en la	Gifts will be given at
fiesta.	the party.

Participles

Present Participles
The Spanish present participle is equivalent to the English *-ing* ending. It is formed

by dropping the **-ar** from **-ar** verbs and adding **-ando** to the infinitive stem:

hablar (to speak) → **hablando** (speaking)

or by dropping the **-er** or **-ir** from **-er** and **-ir** verbs and adding **-iendo** to the infinitive stem:

comer (to eat) → **comiendo** (eating)

Common deviations from this pattern are listed below. Note that stem changes (page 90) often remain in the present participle.

20
mrv

COMMON IRREGULAR PRESENT PARTICIPLES

caer to fall	**cayendo** falling
creer to believe	**creyendo** believing
decir to tell	**diciendo** telling
dormir to sleep	**durmiendo** sleeping
ir to go	**yendo** going
leer to read	**leyendo** reading
mentir to lie	**mintiendo** lying
morir to die	**muriendo** dying
oír to hear	**oyendo** hearing
pedir to ask (for)	**pidiendo** asking (for)
poder to be able	**pudiendo** being able
preferir to prefer	**prefiriendo** preferring
reír to laugh	**riendo** laughing
seguir to follow	**siguiendo** following
sentir to feel	**sintiendo** feeling
ser to be	**siendo** being
servir to serve	**sirviendo** serving
traer to bring	**trayendo** bringing
venir to come	**viniendo** coming

**20
mrv**

Past Participles

The past participle is the Spanish equivalent to the English *-ed*, *-en*, etc. endings. It is formed

by dropping the **-ar** from **-ar** verbs and adding **-ado** to the infinitive stem:

nevar (to snow) → **nevado** (snowed)

or by dropping the **-er** or **-ir** from **-er** and **-ir** verbs and adding **-ido** to the infinitive stem:

surtir (to supply) → **surtido** (supplied)

The past participle, with the auxiliary verb **haber,** forms the perfect verb tenses (see page 73). Some past participles also function as adjectives (see page 28).

The past participle does not need to agree in gender or number when it is used as a verb.

He comido la manzana.   I *have eaten* the apple.

It does need to agree in gender and number when it is used as an adjective.

la manzana comida   the *eaten* apple

Common deviations from the general formation pattern are listed below. Note that when the **-ido** is attached to a verb stem ending in a vowel, an accent is placed over the **i** for emphasis.

traer to bring → **traído** brought

```
              COMMON IRREGULAR PAST PARTICIPLES

        abrir  to open                abierto  opened
        caer  to fall                 caído  fallen
        creer  to believe             creído  believed
        cubrir  to cover              cubierto  covered
        decir  to tell                dicho  told
        describir  to describe        descrito  described
        escribir  to write            escrito  written
        freír  to fry                 frito  fried
        hacer  to do, to make         hecho  made
        ir  to go                     ido  gone
        leer  to read                 leído  read
        morir  to die                 muerto  died
        oír  to hear                  oído  heard
        poner  to put                 puesto  put
        reír  to laugh                reído  laughed
        romper  to break              roto  broken
        ser  to be                    sido  been
        traer  to bring               traído  brought
        ver  to see                   visto  seen
        volver  to return             vuelto  returned
```

**20
mrv**

Tense Relationship in Clauses

The following are some general rules about tense relationship.

If the main clause is in the present or future tense, the dependent clause is in the present subjunctive or the present perfect subjunctive.

Yo *quiero* que ella *hable*   I *want* her to *speak* to Juan.
con Juan.

If the main clause is in a past tense or conditional tense, the dependent clause is in the imperfect subjunctive or the past perfect subjunctive.

Yo *cantaría* ... si Juan   I *would sing* ... if Juan
***viniera* a la fiesta.**   *would come* to the party.

If the *if* clause is in the present indicative or the future tense, the *then* clause is in the future tense.

Si *puedo* creerte, *estaré*   If I *can* believe you,
muy contento.   I *will be* very happy.

If the *if* clause is in the imperfect subjunctive or past perfect subjunctive, the *then* clause is in the conditional or conditional perfect tense.

Si *tuviera* dinero, yo *iría*   If I *had* money,
a México.   I *would go* to Mexico.
Si *hubiéramos encontra-*   If we *had found* a doctor,
do* un médico, él *no ha-   he *would not have died.*
bría muerto.

20
mrv

The Multi-Use Infinitive

The infinitive form of the verb is more functional in Spanish than it is in English. It is used in the following situations.

As an infinitive:

Es necesario *ir* a la   It is necessary *to go* to school.
escuela.

After prepositions (equivalent to the gerund in English):

Después de *mirar* sus notas...	After *looking* at his notes...
Al *salir* de la iglesia...	On *leaving* the church...

As the subject or object of a verb:

***Asistir* al colegio es una obligación.**	*Attending* school is an obligation.

In impersonal commands:

No *hablar*.	No talking.

In expressions with the personal **a** (page 47):

Oí *hablar* a Roberto.	I heard Robert *speak*.
Veré *jugar* a los niños.	I will see the children *play*.

With the recent past condition (page 68).

With the near future condition (page 69).

Verbs Using the Infinitives of Other Verbs

**20
mrv**

Often a conjugated form of a verb is combined with an infinitive of another verb to create a desired expression.

***Espero volar* a Francia este verano.**	*I hope to fly* to France *this summer.*

The following verbs can be conjugated and followed by an infinitive without a preposition:

aconsejar to advise	**ordenar** to arrange to
deber to ought to	**permitir** to allow to
dejar to allow to	**poder** to be able to
desear to desire to	**preferir** to prefer to
esperar to hope to	**prohibir** to prohibit
hacer to force to	**prometer** to promise to
mandar to order to	**querer** to want to
necesitar to need to	**saber** to know how to
oír to hear	**ver** to see to

With some verbs, a preposition is needed to link the conjugated verb and the infinitive.

Terminó de pintar la cerca.   *He finished painting* the fence.

The following verbs can be conjugated and linked to an infinitive with the preposition indicated:

acostumbrar(se) *a* to get used to
aprender *a* to learn to
aspirar *a* to aspire to
ayudar *a* to help to
comenzar *a* to begin to
decidir(se) *a* to decide to
dedicar(se) *a* to devote oneself to
detener(se) *a* to stop to
empezar *a* to begin to
enseñar *a* to teach to
invitar *a* to invite to
ir *a* to be going to
negar(se) *a* to refuse to
obligar *a* to compel to
preparar(se) *a* to prepare to
principar(se) *a* to start to
regresar *a* to return to
salir *a* to go out to
venir *a* to come to
volver *a* to return to
contar *con* to count on

soñar *con* to dream about
preocupar(se) *con* to be concerned with
acabar *de* to have just
acordar(se) *de* to remember to
alegrar(se) *de* to be happy to/with
cansar *de* to tire of
dejar *de* to stop/fail to
haber *de* to be supposed to
ocupar(se) *de* to be busy with
olvidar(se) *de* to forget to
preocupar(se) *de* to be concerned about
terminar *de* to finish
tratar *de* to try to
confiar *en* to trust to
consentir *en* to consent to
consistir *en* to consist of
convenir *en* to agree to
empeñar(se) *en* to persist in
insistir *en* to insist on
quedar *en* to agree on
tardar *en* to delay in

Being: *Ser* and *Estar*

Ser is used to express essence or inherent quality.

Definition:

Es una piñata.   It is a piñata.

Material:

Es de madera.   It is wooden.

Ownership:

Son de Sarah.   They are Sarah's.

Color:

Son amarillos.   They are yellow.

Profession:

Es abogado.   He is an attorney.

Characteristic or permanent condition:

Es guapo.   He is handsome.

Origin:

Es de México.   She is from Mexico.

Location of temporary event:

La fiesta es en la casa   The party is at Maria's house.
de María.

Time and date (page 96):

Son las dos.   It is 2:00.

With the past participle to form the passive voice (page 81):

La catedral fue construí-   The cathedral was built
da de piedra.   of stone.

With impersonal expressions (page 79):

Es posible que...   It's possible that...

20
mrv

Estar is used for temporary conditions.

Location:

> **Estamos en los Estados**   We are in the United States.
> **Unidos.**

Position:

> **Están parados.**   They are stopped.

Condition:

> **Estamos enfermos.**   We are sick.

With the present participle to construct the present and past progressive tenses (pages 81, 82):

> **Estoy leyendo ahora.**   I am reading now.

When used with certain adjectives, **ser** and **estar** change the meaning of the word:

Es aburrido. He is boring.	**Está aburrido.** He is bored.
Es cansado. He is tiresome.	**Está cansado.** He is tired.
Es divertido. He is amusing.	**Está divertido.** He is amused.
Es enfermo. He is sickly.	**Está enfermo.** He is sick.
Es guapo. He is handsome.	**Está guapo.** He is dressed up.
Es listo. He is sharp.	**Está listo.** He is ready.
Es triste. He is dull.	**Está triste.** He is sad.
Es vivo. He is alert.	**Está vivo.** He is alive.

20
mrv

Having: *Tener*

In combination with the listed words, the verb **tener** expresses:

> **tener ___ años** to be ___ years old
> **tener calor** to be hot
> **tener hambre** to be hungry
> **tener sed** to be thirsty
> **tener suerte** to be lucky
> **tener miedo** to be afraid
> **tener vergüenza** to be embarrassed
> **tener sueño** to be sleepy
> **tener prisa** to be in a rush

tener razón to be right
tener cuidado to be careful
tener éxito to be successful
tener lugar to take place

Tener, with **que** and an infinitive, is also used to express obligation.

Yo tengo que estudiar   I have to study more.
más.

Tener is also used to describe maladies just as *to have* does in English.

tener gripe to have the flu
tener catarro to have a cold
tener fiebre to have a fever
tener tos to have a cough
tener dolor de cabeza to have a headache
tener dolor de estómago to have a stomachache
tener dolor de garganta to have a sore throat
tener dolor de muelas to have a toothache
tener dolor de oídos to have an earache
tener dolor de espalda to have a backache

Auxiliary Verb *Haber*

The following forms of the auxiliary verb **haber** occur frequently:

**20
mrv**

Present	**hay**	there is/are
Imperfect	**había**	there was/were
Preterite	**hubo**	there was/were
Present Perfect	**ha habido**	there has/have been
Present Subjunctive	**haya**	there may be
Imperfect Subjunctive	**hubiese**	there might be
Near Future	**va a haber**	there is going to be
Future	**habrá**	there will be

Also: **debe haber**   there should/must be
         puede haber   there could be
         tiene que haber   there has/have to be
         hay que + infinitive   it is necessary that

Also see discussion of the perfect tenses beginning on page 72.

Stem Changes and Spelling Changes in Verbs

The spelling of many Spanish verbs changes upon conjugation. Vowel alterations in verb stems are called stem changes. These normally apply to all but the first and second person plural forms in the present tense and some also apply to the present participle. There are three standard stem-changing rules that all stem changing verbs follow.

1. In some **-ir** verbs, the **e** in the stem changes to **i**.

PEDIR TO ASK FOR			
In the Present Indicative		*In the Present Subjunctive*	
pide	**pedimos**	**pida**	**pidamos**
pides	pedís	**pidas**	pidáis
pide	**piden**	**pida**	**pidan**
Present Participle: **pidiendo**			

Other **e → i** stem-changing verbs include: **medir** *(to measure),* **repetir** *(to repeat),* **servir** *(to serve),* and **vestir** *(to dress).*

2. In some verbs, the **e** in the stem changes to **ie**.

QUERER TO WANT			
In the Present Indicative		*In the Present Subjunctive*	
quiero	**queremos**	**quiera**	**queramos**
quieres	queréis	**quieras**	queráis
quiere	**quieren**	**quiera**	**quieran**

Other **e → ie** stem-changing verbs include **cerrar** *(to close),* **comenzar** *(to begin),* **convertir** *(to convert),* **despertar** *(to awaken),* **empezar** *(to begin),* **entender** *(to understand),* **mentir** *(to lie),*

20
mrv

pensar *(to think)*, **perder** *(to lose)*, **preferir** *(to prefer)*, **sentir** *(to feel)*, **tener** *(to have)*, and **venir** *(to come)*.

3. In some verbs, the **o** or **u** in the stem changes to **ue**:

MOSTRAR TO SHOW			
In the Present Indicative		*In the Present Subjunctive*	
muestro	**mostramos**	**muestre**	**mostremos**
muestras	mostráis	**muestres**	**mostréis**
muestra	**muestran**	**muestre**	**muestren**

Other **o** or **u** → **ue** stem-changing verbs include **almorzar** *(to eat lunch)*, **contar** *(to count)*, **costar** *(to cost)*, **dormir** *(to sleep)*, **jugar** *(to play)*, **morir** *(to die)*, **poder** *(to be able)*, **recordar** *(to remember)*, and **volver** *(to turn)*.

Other forms of spelling change follow general spelling rules—for example, **z** changes to **c** before **e** and **i**—or they are more idiosyncratic in nature.

20
mrv

21 | *Summary (sum)*

	-ar Verbs		**-er, -ir** Verbs	
Present Indicative (page 58)				
1st Person	-o	-amos	-o	-emos, -imos
2nd Person *(fam.)*	-as	-áis	-es	-éis, ís
3rd Person, 2nd *(form.)*	-a	-an	-e	-en
Present Subjunctive (page 60)				
1st Person	-e	-emos	-a	-amos
2nd Person *(fam.)*	-es	-éis	-as	-áis
3rd Person, 2nd *(form.)*	-e	-en	-a	-an
Preterite (page 64)				
1st Person	-é	-amos	-í	-imos
2nd Person *(fam.)*	-aste	-asteis	-iste	-isteis
3rd Person, 2nd *(form.)*	-ó	-aron	-ió	-ieron
Imperfect Indicative (page 65)				
1st Person	-aba	-ábamos	-ía	-íamos
2nd Person *(fam.)*	-abas	-abais	-ías	-íais
3rd Person, 2nd *(form.)*	-aba	-aban	-ía	-ían
Imperfect Subjunctive (page 66)				
For all verbs				
1st Person	-ra	-ramos	-se	-semos
2nd Person *(fam.)*	-ras	-rais OR	-ses	-seis
3rd Person, 2nd *(form.)*	-ra	-raran	-se	-sen
Future (page 69)				
Add to the infinitive:				
1st Person		-é	-emos	
2nd Person *(fam.)*		-ás	-éis	
3rd Person, 2nd *(form.)*		-á	-án	

(continued)

21
sum

Conditional (page 71)

Add to the infinitive:

1st Person	**-ía**	**-íamos**
2nd Person *(fam.)*	**-ías**	-íais
3rd Person, 2nd *(form.)*	**-ía**	**-ían**

OTHER TENSE CONDITIONS

Present Progressive (page 59)

Present of **estar** + *Present Participle*

Imperfect Progressive (page 68)

Imperfect of **estar** + *Present Participle*

Recent Past Condition (page 68)

Form of **acabar** + **de** + *Infinitive*

Near Future Condition (page 69)

Form of **ir** + **a** + *Infinitive*

21
sum

22 Telling Time
At a Particular Time
Expressing Duration
Days, Months, and Seasons

23 Counting and Converting
The Numbers
Basic Math Expressions
Conversions of Weights and Measures

24 Useful Spanish
Members of the Family
Parts of the Body
Countries and Nationalities
Making Comparisons:
Comparatives and Superlatives
Writing a Letter in Spanish

25 Common Expressions
Exclamations
General Conversation
Time and Temperature
On the Road
Signs in Public Places
In a Hotel
Going Shopping
Eating Out
In Need of Assistance
Other Useful Terms and Phrases

Functional Expressions

The other sections of this book are designed to explain the various parts of speech and the rules governing their use and formation. This section on functional expressions will show how these rules are applied in specific contexts. From telling time to ordering a meal to asking for help, the rest of **Más fácil** illustrates how Spanish is used in practical, everyday situations.

22 | *Telling Time* (tet)

In Spanish, there is no word that is equivalent to the word *o'clock*. When telling the time, only the number of the hour is needed. A feminine definite article precedes the number of the hour, and the word for *hour* itself **(la hora)** is omitted.

> **a las siete** at seven o'clock
> **a la una** at one o'clock

Time is generally expressed with a form of the verb **ser** *(to be)*.

¿Qué hora es?	What time is it?
Es la una.	It is 1:00.
Son las dos.	It is 2:00.

From the hour to half past the hour, minutes are expressed with **y** *(and)*.

Es la una *y cinco.*	It is 1:05.
Es la una *y diez.*	It is 1:10.
Es la una *y cuarto.*	It is 1:15.
Es la una *y media.*	It is 1:30.

Between half past the hour and the hour, there are various ways to express time.

Son las dos *menos veintinueve.*	It is 1:31.

Son *veintinueve* (minu-tos) *para* las dos.[1]	
Faltan *veintinueve para* las dos.	It is 1:31.
Es la una *y treinta y uno*.	
Son las dos *menos cuarto*.	It is 1:45.
Es un *cuarto para* las dos.	

After one o'clock the third person plural of **ser (son)** is used to express the hour.

Son las tres *y veinte*.	It is 3:20.

Noon and midnight are expressed without an article.

Es *mediodía*.	It is noon.
Es *medianoche*.	It is midnight.

The imperfect indicative tense of the verb **ser** is used to tell time in the past.

***Eran* las once cuando fui a casa.**	It *was* eleven o'clock when I went home.

The future tense is used to tell time in the future or to give the approximate time.

***Serán* las tres y media.**	It *will be* OR It *probably is* 3:30.

The designators A.M. and P.M. are not used in spoken Spanish. The preposition **de** is used with the three times of day—morning, afternoon, and night.

Son las diez *de la mañana*.	{ It's 10:00 A.M. It's 10:00 in the morning.
Es la una y media *de la tarde*.	It's 1:30 P.M. (before nightfall)
Son las nueve y ocho *de la noche*.	It's 9:08 P.M.

---

[1] The word for minutes (**minutos**) is occasionally included.

At a Particular Time

The preposition **a** *(at)* is used to indicate a specific time.

¿A qué hora vas al cine?	What time are you going to the movies?
Voy *a* las cuatro y media en punto.	I'm going at 4:30 sharp.
Llego al trabajo *a* eso de las siete.	I arrive at work at about 7:00.

The preposition **por** *(for)* is used to express *at* or *in* when no hour is given.

Trabaja *por* la tarde y juega *por* la noche.	He works in the afternoon and plays at night.

Specific Points in Time

last night **anoche**
yesterday **ayer**
yesterday morning **ayer por la mañana**
day before yesterday **anteayer**
last week **la semana pasada**
now **ahora**
someday **algún día**
soon **pronto**
later **más tarde**
today **hoy**
this morning **esta mañana**
this afternoon **esta tarde**
tonight **esta noche**
at midnight **a medianoche**
tomorrow **mañana**
tomorrow morning **mañana por la mañana**
day after tomorrow **pasado mañana**
this weekend **este fin de semana**
next weekend **la semana que viene**

22
tet

Expressing Duration

Hace, present tense of the verb **hacer**, is used to express what has been happening over a specific period of time.

hace + *length of time* + **que** + *present tense*

Hace diez años **que** *vivimos* **aquí.**	We *have been living* here *for ten years.*

The literal translation is: It makes ten years that we live here.

Without **que**, **hace** is used to express the concept of *ago* when used with a verb in the past tense.

Vivieron **en México** *hace* **diez años.**	They *lived* in Mexico ten years *ago.*
Fui hace **dos días.**	I *went* two days *ago.*

Hacer in the imperfect tense is used to express what had been happening.

hacía + *length of time* + **que** + *imperfect tense*

Hacía dos meses **que** *estaba* **enferma.**	She *had been* sick *for two months.*

The literal translation is: It made two months that she was sick.

Days, Months, and Seasons

Days of the Week

Monday **lunes**
Tuesday **martes**
Wednesday **miércoles**
Thursday **jueves**
Friday **viernes**
Saturday **sábado**
Sunday **domingo**

- The days of the week are not capitalized.
- All days of the week are masculine.
- A definite article is used to express *on*.

Vendré *el* **lunes.**	I will come *on* Monday.

22
tet

The plural masculine definite article **los** is used with repeat occurrences.

El programa lo ponen en la televisión *los* lunes.	The program is on television on Mondays.

Months of the Year

January **enero**	July **julio**
February **febrero**	August **agosto**
March **marzo**	September **septiembre**
April **abril**	October **octubre**
May **mayo**	November **noviembre**
June **junio**	December **diciembre**

* The months of the year are not capitalized.
* All months are masculine.
* To express a date, the singular masculine article **el** precedes the day, and the preposition **de** precedes the month and the year.

el primero *de* junio[1]	June 1st
el cuatro *de* julio *de* mil novecientos setenta y seis	July 4, 1976
What's today's *date?*	**¿Qué *fecha* es hoy? ¿Cuál es la *fecha* de hoy?**
It's the 2nd of November.	**Es el dos *de* noviembre.**

The Four Seasons

spring **la primavera**
summer **el verano**
fall **el otoño**
winter **el invierno**

22
tet

---

[1] **Primero** *(first)* is the only ordinal adjective used with dates.

23 | Counting and Converting (coc)

The Numbers

0 cero	20 veinte	700 setecientos(as)
1 uno[1]	21 veintiuno[2]	800 ochocientos(as)
2 dos	30 treinta	900 novecientos(as)
3 tres	31 treinta y uno	1000 mil[4]
4 cuatro	40 cuarenta	1500 mil quinientos
5 cinco	50 cincuenta	1990 mil novecientos
6 seis	60 sesenta	noventa
7 siete	70 setenta	2500 dos mil quinientos
8 ocho	80 ochenta	5000 cinco mil
9 nueve	90 noventa	100.000[5] cien mil
10 diez	100 cien	1.000.000 un millón
11 once	101 ciento uno	100.000.000 cien
12 doce	110 ciento diez	millones
13 trece	120 ciento veinte	
14 catorce	130 ciento treinta	
15 quince	200 doscientos(as)[3]	
16 dieciséis[2]	300 trescientos(as)	
17 diecisiete	400 cuatrocientos(as)	
18 dieciocho	500 quinientos(as)	
19 diecinueve	600 seiscientos(as)	

**23
coc**

---

[1] **uno** drops the **-o** before a masculine noun.

[2] Sometimes written as **diez y seis, veinte y uno**, etc.

[3] Only the hundreds and the ordinal numbers (page 30) have to agree in gender and number.

[4] **Mil** is never pluralized and never takes the indefinite pronoun. This is *not* the case with **millón**.

[5] Note that units of thousands are separated by a period in Spanish, not a comma. In Spanish, the comma is used in place of the decimal point.

Basic Math Expressions

más, y plus (+)
menos minus (−)

por times (×)
dividido por divided by (÷)

$6 + 2 = 8$ **Seis y dos son ocho.**
$10 − 3 = 7$ **Diez menos tres son siete.**
$2 × 2 = 4$ **Dos por dos son cuatro.**
$12 ÷ 4 = 3$ **Doce dividido por cuatro son tres.**

Conversions of Weights and Measures

Multiplique Multiply		**por** by[1]	**para convertir a** to convert to	
Peso	Weight			
la onza	ounce	28,350[2]	**el gramo**	gram
la libra	pound	0,454	**el kilogramo**	kilogram
la tonelada	ton	0,907	**la tonelada métrica**	metric ton
Capacidad	Volume			
la onza	ounce	29,563	**el mililitro**	mililiter
la taza	cup	0,236	**el litro**	liter
la pinta	pint	0,473	**el litro**	
el cuarto	quart	0,946	**el litro**	
el galón	gallon	3,785	**el litro**	
Longitud	Length			
la pulgada	inch	2,540	**el centímetro**	centimeter
el pie	foot	30,480	**el centímetro**	
		0,305	**el metro**	meter
la yarda	yard	0,914	**el metro**	
la milla	mile	1,609	**el kilómetro**	kilometer

23
coc

---

[1] If converting the other way, from metric units, divide the given number of metric units by the factor to find the comparable number of American units.
[2] In Spanish, decimals are indicated by a comma, not a period.

24 | *Useful Spanish* (usp)

Members of the Family

los parientes		relatives
el padre	la madre	father/mother
el esposo	la esposa	husband/wife
los padres		parents
el hermano	la hermana	brother/sister
el hijo	la hija	son/daughter
el niño	la niña	child
el abuelo	la abuela	grandfather/grandmother
el nieto	la nieta	grandson/granddaughter
el tío	la tía	uncle/aunt
el sobrino	la sobrina	nephew/niece
el primo	la prima	cousin

(Step Relationships)

el padrastro	la madrastra	stepfather/stepmother
el hijastro	la hijastra	stepson/stepdaughter
el hermanastro	la hermanastra	stepbrother/stepsister

(In-Laws)

el suegro	la suegra	father-in-law/mother-in-law
el yerno	la nuera	son-in-law/daughter-in-law
el cuñado	la cuñada	brother-in-law/sister-in-law

(Other)

el padrino	la madrina	godfather/godmother
el ahijado	la ahijada	godson/goddaughter
el viudo	la viuda	widower/widow
el huérfano	la huérfana	orphan

24
usp

(Family Status)

adoptivo	adopted
soltero	single
comprometido	engaged
casado	married
divorciado	divorced

Parts of the Body

ankle **el tobillo**	foot **el pie**	mouth **la boca**
arm **el brazo**	forehead **la frente**	neck **el cuello**
back **la espalda**	hair **el pelo**	nose **la nariz**
blood **la sangre**	hand **la mano**	shoulder **el hombro**
body **el cuerpo**	head **la cabeza**	skin **la piel**
bone **el hueso**	heart **el corazón**	stomach **el estómago**
brain **el cerebro**	heel **el talón**	throat **la garganta**
chest **el pecho**	hip **la cadera**	thumb **el pulgar**
chin **la barbilla**	jaw **la quijada**	toe **el dedo del pie**
ear **el oído**	knee **la rodilla**	tongue **la lengua**
elbow **el codo**	leg **la pierna**	tooth **el diente**
eye **el ojo**	lip **el labio**	waist **la cintura**
face **la cara**	liver **el hígado**	wrist **la muñeca**
finger **el dedo**	lung **el pulmón**	

Countries and Nationalities

Country		Nationality[1]
Argentina	**Argentina**	**argentino**
Bolivia	**Bolivia**	**boliviano**
Brazil	**Brasil**	**brasileño**
Chile	**Chile**	**chileno**

---

[1] Nationalities, like other descriptive adjectives (page 24), must agree in gender and number with the nouns they modify. The masculine singular forms are shown above. If the masculine singular form ends in a consonant, **-a** is added to form the feminine. In addition:

- Nationalities are not capitalized.
- Adjectives of nationality always follow the noun (**la comida cubana** the cuban food).
- The masculine singular form of the nationality is used to refer to the language of the country but requires the definite article **el** (**el ruso** the Russian language).

China	**China**	chino
Columbia	**Colombia**	colombiano
Costa Rica	**Costa Rica**	costarricense
Cuba	**Cuba**	cuban
Dominican Republic	**la República Dominicana**	dominicano
Ecuador	**Ecuador**	ecuatoriano
El Salvador	**El Salvador**	salvadoreño
England	**Inglaterra**	inglés
France	**Francia**	francés
Germany	**Alemania**	alemán
Guatemala	**Guatemala**	guatemalteco
Honduras	**Honduras**	hondureño
Italy	**Italia**	italiano
Japan	**Japón**	japonés
Mexico	**México**	mexicano
Nicaragua	**Nicaragua**	nicaragüense
Panama	**Panama**	panameño
Paraguay	**Paraguay**	paraguayo
Peru	**Perú**	peruano
Portugal	**Portugal**	portugués
Puerto Rico	**Puerto Rico**	puertorriqueño
Russia	**Rusia**	ruso
Spain	**España**	español
United States	**Estados Unidos**	norteamericano
Uruguay	**Uruguay**	uruguayo
Venezuela	**Venezuela**	venezolano

Making Comparisons: Comparatives and Superlatives

COMPARATIVES

más... que...   more... than...

> **Él está *más* feliz *que* triste.**   He is *more* happy *than* sad.
>
> **Ella estudia *más que* Nora.**   She studies *more than* Nora.

24
usp

más... de...	more... than...

With numbers, in affirmative sentences only, use **de** instead of **que**.

Tengo *más de* cinco dólares.	I have *more than* 5 dollars.

de lo (la/los/las) que...	more... than...

If two clauses are being compared, use **de lo(la/los/las) que**.

Ese trabajo está *más* difícil *de lo que* Ud. cree.	That job is *more* difficult *than* you think.

menos... que...	less... than...

Marcos come *menos que* Jorge.	Marcos eats *less than* Jorge.

tan... como...	as... as...

María es *tan* bonita *como* Carmen.	Maria is *as* beautiful *as* Carmen.

tanto... como...	as (quantity)... as...

Tuvo *tantas* cosas *como* su amigo.	He had *as many* things *as* his friend.

Note that **tanto(a/os/as)** must agree in gender and number with the nouns they modify.

cuanto más (menos)...	*the more* (less)...
tanto más (menos)...	*the more* (less)...

Cuanto más atención recibe, tanto más necesita.	The more attention she gets, the more she needs.

SUPERLATIVES

el (la) más... (de)	most...

Paula es *la más alta* de la familia.	Paula is *the tallest* in the family.

24
usp

| el (la) menos... (de) | least... |

Jaime es *el menos* dedicado. — Jaime is *the least dedicated.*

With superlatives, the definite article modifies the compared noun. However, note that the definite article is *not* used at all to express the superlative of an adverb.

| *el* estudiante *más* inteligente | *the* smart*est* student |
| Habló más tristemente. | He spoke most sadly. |

| el (la) mayoría de... | most... (literally: the majority of...) |

| la *mayoría de* las mujeres... | *most* women... |

THE ABSOLUTE SUPERLATIVE

The absolute superlative, which expresses *most* or *very,* is formed with adjectives ending in **-ísimo(a/os/as) Roberto es guapísimo.** *Roberto is very handsome.* Some adjectives undergo a spelling change when **-ísimo** is added.

antiguo old	**antiquísimo** very old
bueno good	**bonísimo** very good
fuerte strong	**fortísimo** very strong
nuevo new	**novísimo** very new
rico rich	**riquísimo** very rich

IRREGULAR COMPARATIVES

bueno(a) good	**malo(a)** bad
mejor (que) better	**peor (que)** worse
el (la) mejor (de) best	**el (la) peor (de)** worst

joven young	**viejo(a)** old
menor (que) younger	**mayor (que)** older
el (la) menor (de) youngest	**el (la) mayor (de)** oldest

pequeño(a) small	**grande** large
menor (que) smaller	**mayor (que)** larger
el (la) menor (de) smallest	**el (la) mayor (de)** largest

24
usp

bajo(a) low			**alto(a)** high	
inferior lower			**superior** higher	
ínfimo(a) lowest			**supremo(a)** highest	

Note that all comparative/superlative adjectives may be made plural: **mejores, peores, menores, mayores, ínfimos(as)**, and **supremos(as)**.

Writing a Letter in Spanish

señor	**Sr.**	Mister Mr.	**Calle c./**	Street
señora	**Sra.**	Mrs.	**Avenida**	Avenue
señorita	**Srta.**	Miss	**Camino**	Road
don	**D.**	Sir	**Plaza**	Plaza
doña	**Dª.**	Madam	**Apartado**	P.O. Box

The following may be used as a model for writing a business letter in Spanish.

Editorial Bilingüe de España S.A.
Avenida de España, 1410
14004 Madrid
SPAIN   4 de enero de 1993

Sr. (Sra.) Urbina
c./ San José, 18
Grecia
COSTA RICA

Estimado(a) Señor(a): *Dear Sir (Madam):*
Muy Señor(a) mío(a):
Muy estimado(a) Señor(a):
Muy Señores míos: *Dear Sirs:*

[body of letter]

Atentamente,
Cordialmente,
Saludos,
Sinceramente,

[Your Name]

---

25 | Common Expressions (coe)

Exclamations

¡Qué...! What a...!

> **¡Qué lastima!** What a shame!
> **¡Qué mujer!** What a woman!
> **¡Qué clase más aburrida!** What a boring class!

¡Tal...! Such a...!

> **¡Tal molestia!** Such a bother!
> **¡Tal buen niño!** Such a good boy!
> **¡Tal lugar!** Such a place!

Here are some other examples of exclamation.

> **¡Caramba!** My goodness!
> **¡Cuánto lo siento!** I'm so sorry!
> **¡Cuánto me alegro (de que...)!** I'm so glad (that...)!
> **¡Cómo no!** Of course! Certainly!
> **¡Fantástico!** Great!
> **¡Ni modo!** No way!
> **¡No hay problema!** There's no problem!
> **¡No me diga!** You don't say!
> **¡No puede ser!** It can't be!
> **¡Oiga!** Listen!
> **¡Qué bueno!** Good!
> **¡Qué gusto!** What a pleasure!

**25
coe**

¡Qué pesado! How boring!
¡Qué te diviertas! Have fun!
¡Qué tontería! How ridiculous!
¡Qué va! No way!
¡Socorro! Help!

General Conversation

Hello! **¡Hola!**
Good morning. **Buenos días.**
Good afternoon. **Buenas tardes.**
Good evening. **Buenas noches.**
Pleased to meet you. **Mucho gusto.**
Come in! **¡Adelante!**
How are you? **¿Cómo está Ud.?**
How do you feel? **¿Cómo se siente Ud.?**
Fine, thank you. **Bien, gracias.**
And you? **¿Y Ud.? ¿Y tú?**
So-so. **Así, así.**

What's going on? **¿Qué hay?**
What's happening? **¿Qué pasa?**
How did it go? **¿Cómo le fue?**
What's new? **¿Qué hay de nuevo?**
What's up? How goes it? **¿Qué tal?**

Excuse me. **Con permiso.**
Pardon me. **Perdóneme.**
My name is... **Me llamo...**
What's your name? **¿Cómo se llama Ud.?**
Where are you from? **¿De dónde es Ud.?**
Where are you going? **¿Adónde va?**

Do you speak English? **¿Habla Ud. inglés?**
How do you say...? **¿Cómo se dice...?**

What do you call...? **¿Cómo se llama...?**

What is this? **¿Qué es esto?**

What are you saying? **¿Cómo dices?**

Please write it. **Escríbalo, por favor.**

Repeat, please. **Repita, por favor.**

Speak more slowly, please. **Hable más despacio, por favor.**

What did you say? **¿Qué dijo Ud.?**

What do you mean? **¿Qué quiere decir?**

What does the word ... mean? **¿Qué significa la palabra ...?**

I cannot find that word in my dictionary. **No encuentro esa palabra en mi diccionario.**

What do you think (if...)? **Qué le parece (si...)?**

I think so. **Creo que sí.**

I don't think so. **Creo que no.**

I don't know. **No sé.**

I forgot. **Se me olvidó.**

I agree. **De acuerdo.**

I disagree. **No estoy de acuerdo.**

Do you understand? **¿Entiende?**

I don't understand. **No entiendo.**

I understand but... **Comprendo, pero...**

It depends on... **Depende de...**

Let's see. **A ver.**

Better not. **Mejor no.**

It's not important. **No importa.**

No problem. **No problema.**

How often? **¿Con qué frecuencia?**

Is it true? **¿Es cierto?**

Really? **¿De veras?**

It's true. **Es verdad.**

Of course. **Por supuesto.**

**25
coe**

Please. **Por favor.**

With pleasure. **Con mucho gusto.**

(Many) thanks. **(Muchas) gracias.**

You're welcome. **De nada.**

I'm (very) sorry. **Lo siento (mucho).**

That man is following me. **Ese hombre me está siguiendo.**

Stop following me. **Deje de seguirme.**

Don't bother me. **No me moleste.**

I want to make a phone call. **Quiero llamar por teléfono.**

Just a minute, please. **Un momento, por favor.**

The line is busy. **Está comunicando.**

Go ahead, please. **Hable, por favor.**

Could I speak with Mr. Gonzalez? **¿Podría hablar con el
   señor González?**

How old are you? **¿Cuántos años tiene Ud.?**

I am twenty years old. **Yo tengo veinte años.**

You look nice. **Te ves muy linda.**

You are very kind. **Es muy amable.**

What is your address? **¿Cuál es su dirección?**

Which is your hotel? **¿Cuál es su hotel?**

Are you married? **¿Es casada Ud.?**

How old are your children? **¿Qué edad tienen sus niños?**

What is your phone number? **¿Cuál es su número de
   teléfono?**

25
coe

May I see you tonight? **¿Puedo verle esta noche?**

I want to go to the movies. **Quiero ir al cine.**

We will be back at 11:00. **Volveremos a las once.**

It is a starry night. **El cielo está estrellado.**

I had a good time. **Me divertí mucho.**

We had a great time. **La pasamos muy bien.**

I love you. **Te quiero.**

Are you crazy? **¿Está loco?**

I have to go home. **Tengo que irme a casa.**

Good luck. **Buena suerte.**

Until tomorrow. **Hasta mañana.**

Until later, then. **Hasta luego.**

Until soon. **Hasta pronto.**

Until we see each other. **Hasta la vista.**

Take care. **Cuídate.**

Good-by. **Adiós.**

To bed! **¡A la cama!**

Time and Temperature

What time is it? **¿Qué hora es?**

all day **todo el día**

How much time (has it been)? **¿Cuánto tiempo (hace)?**

have time for **tener tiempo para**

What day is today? **¿Qué día es hoy?**

Today is Friday. **Hoy es viernes.**

Today is the fifth of May. **Hoy es el cinco de mayo.**

What month is it? **¿En qué mes estamos?**

It's April. **Estamos en abril.**

How is the weather? **¿Qué tiempo hace?**

The weather is good. **Hace buen tiempo.**

What will the weather be tomorrow? **¿Qué tiempo hará mañana?**

It's sunny. **Hace sol.**

It is raining. **Está lloviendo.**

It was very windy. **Hacía mucho viento.**

There is a pleasant breeze. **Hace una brisa muy agradable.**

What is the temperature? **¿Qué temperatura hace?**

It is 30 degrees. **Está a treinta grados centígrados.**

It's (very) hot. **Hace (mucho) calor.**

25
coe

It's cool. **Hace fresco.**

It's cold. **Hace frío.**

It was very cold yesterday. **Hacía mucho frío ayer.**

It's snowing. **Está nevando.**

There is a storm. **Hay una tormenta.**

When is high tide? **¿Cuándo está la marea alta?**

On the Road

to travel around the world **darle la vuelta al mundo**

to go abroad **ir al extranjero**

to go on vacation **ir de vacaciones**

to take a trip **hacer un (el) viaje**

on a visit **de visita**

to make reservations **hacer reservaciones**

travel agency **agencia de viajes**

nonstop **sin escala**

one-way **de un sentido**

two-way **de doble sentido**

round trip **ida y vuelta**

to pack a suitcase **hacer la maleta**

to check baggage **entregar el equipaje**

My bags have not arrived. **No ha llegado mi equipaje.**

That is my suitcase. **Eso es mi equipaje.**

I am staying for two months. **Me voy a quedar dos meses.**

Can you tell me how to get to the airport? **¿Puede decirme por dónde se va al aeropuerto?**

Where is the ticket office? **¿Dónde está la oficina de boletos?**

Where do I get the flight to...? **¿De dónde sale el vuelo de...?**

I want to go to Mexico. **Quiero ir a México.**

25
coe

a round-trip ticket to San José **un billete de ida y vuelta para San Jose**

What time does the boat arrive? **¿A qué hora llega el barco?**

What time does the bus leave? **¿A qué hora sale el autobús?**

Is this seat taken? **¿Está ocupado este asiento?**

The train is very fast. **El tren es muy rápido.**

When is the next train to...? **¿Cuándo sale el próximo tren para...?**

When will it arrive? **¿Cuándo llegará?**

How long will we have to wait? **¿Cuánto tiempo tendremos que esperar?**

I have missed my train. **He perdido el tren.**

How do I get out of here? **¿Cómo salgo de aquí?**

Is there another way? **¿Hay alguna otra ruta?**

Here is my passport. **Aquí está mi pasaporte.**

I have lost my passport. **He perdido el pasaporte.**

I have nothing to declare. **No tengo nada que declarar.**

I want to rent a car. **Quiero alquilar un coche.**

Here is my driver's license. **Aquí está mi permiso de conducir.**

Can you show me on the map? **¿Puede indicármelo en el mapa?**

Where can I park the car? **¿Dónde puedo aparcar el coche?**

Are there any sightseeing tours? **¿Hay excursiones turísticas?**

How far is it? **¿Qué distancia hay?**

Can I take pictures? **¿Puedo hacer fotos?**

My camera doesn't work. **Mi cámara no va bien.**

Where is the best view? **¿Desde dónde hay mejor vista?**

to take a walk **dar un paseo**

25
coe

to go for hikes **dar caminatas**

This is a lot of fun. **Es tan divertida.**

I would like to change some money. **Quisiera cambiar dinero.**

May I change money here? **¿Puedo cambiar dinero aquí?**

What is the exchange rate for dollars? **¿A cómo está el dólar?**

Do you accept traveler's checks? **¿Aceptan cheques de viaje?**

Do you sell... guidebooks? **¿Venden... guías del viajero?**

Where is the bathroom? **¿Dónde está el cuarto de baño?**

Where is the toilet? **¿Dónde está el baño?**

I am lost. **Me he perdido.**

Turn left. **Doble a la izquierda.**

Turn right. **Doble a la derecha.**

Go straight ahead. **Siga derecho.**

You have to turn around. **Tiene que dar la vuelta.**

Signs in Public Places

Abierto	Open
Acceso a los andenes	To the Trains
Aduana	Customs
Alto	Stop
Ascensor	Elevator
Caballeros	Men's Restroom
Caja	Cash Register
Cerrado	Closed
Completo	Full
Consigna	Luggage Room
Damas	Ladies' Restroom
Despacio	Slow
Desviación	Detour
Empuje	Push

25
coe

Entrada	Entrance
Estacionamiento prohibido	No Parking
Libre	Vacant
No tocar	Do Not Touch
Ocupado	Taken or Engaged
Peligro	Danger
Pinta	Wet Paint
Policía	Police
Privada	Private
Prohibido bañarse	No Bathing
Prohibido el paso	No Entry
Prohibido fumar	No Smoking
Prohibido pisar la hierba	Keep Off the Grass
Salida	Exit
Servicio incluido	Service Included
Servicios	Toilets
Silencio	Silence
Teléfono	Telephone
Tirar	Pull

In a Hotel

Do you have a room with a view? **¿Tiene una habitación con vista?**

Do you have a room with a bed, a desk, and a shower? **¿Tiene una habitación de una cama con escritorio y ducha?**

Do you serve meals? **¿Sirven comidas?**

Could I see some rooms? **¿Podría ver algunos cuartos?**

I would like a single room. **Quisiera una habitación individual.**

How much is the room per night? **¿Cuánto es la habitación por noche?**

I want to stay for one week. **Quiero quedarme una semana.**

The view is magnificent. **La vista es magnífica.**

Is there a swimming pool? **¿Hay piscina?**

Is the voltage 110 or 220? **¿La corriente es de ciento diez o de doscientos veinte?**

25
coe

Is there a car or bus into town? **¿Hay algún auto o autobús al centro de la ciudad?**

Could you look after these bags? **¿Podría cuidarme estas maletas?**

Can I put this in the safe? **¿Puedo dejar esto en la caja fuerte?**

Can you develop this film? **¿Puede revelar esta película?**

Can I have another blanket? **¿Puede darme otra manta?**

Can you wash these clothes? **¿Puede lavar esta ropa?**

I would like to cash a check. **Quisiera hacer efectivo un cheque.**

How much is a letter to the United States? **¿Qué franquero lleva una carta a los Estados Unidos?**

Can you order me a taxi? **¿Puede llamarme un taxi?**

Any messages? **¿Hay mensajes?**

I would like to make a phone call to... **Quisiera hacer una llamada telefónica a...**

The toilet won't flush. **El inodoro no funciona.**

There is no hot water. **No hay agua caliente.**

I have no towels in the room. **No tengo toallas en la habitación.**

The air conditioner is not working. **El aire acondicionado no funciona.**

I would like to see the manager. **Quisiera ver al director.**

How much do I owe? **¿Cuánto le debo?**

There is a mistake here. **Hay un error aquí.**

Could you give me an itemized bill? **¿Puede darme una factura detallada?**

25 coe

Going Shopping

to go shopping **ir de compras**

How may I serve you? **¿En qué le puedo servir?**

I'm just looking. **Sólo estoy mirando.**

I would like to see... **Quisiera ver...**

I'm looking for a black leather skirt. **Busco una falda de cuero negro.**

Can I try it on? **¿Puedo probármelo?**

A mirror, please. **Un espejo, por favor.**

Bring me that. **Tráigame eso.**

That jacket fits you well. **Esa chaqueta le queda bien.**

It doesn't fit. **No me queda bien.**

I don't like it. **No me gusta.**

My size is... **Mi talla es...**

Do you have a bigger size? **¿Tiene una talla más grande?**

Do you have it in another color? **¿Lo tiene en otro color?**

Do you have something in green? **¿Tiene algo en verde?**

Do you have anything cheaper? **¿Tiene algo más barato?**

for sale **de venta**

I like this one. **Me gusta esto.**

I want this. **Quiero esto.**

I will take it. **Me lo llevo.**

Do you have American newspapers? **¿Tiene periódicos americanos?**

What is the price? **¿Qué precio tiene?**

How much does it cost? **¿Cuánto cuesta?**

I don't have enough money. **No tengo dinero suficiente.**

Do you take credit cards? **¿Aceptan tarjetas de crédito?**

**25
coe**

I will not bargain. **No negociaré.**

I will buy it at another store. **Lo compraré a una tienda otra.**

You have given me the wrong change. **Me ha dado usted mal el cambio.**

Here is something for your assistance. **Aquí tiene algo por su ayuda.**

Eating Out

What time does the restaurant close? **¿A qué hora cierra el restaurante?**

I am trying to diet. **Estoy tratando de estar a dieta.**

Should we reserve a table? **¿Será necesario reservar mesa?**

I'd like a table for two, please. **Quisiera una mesa para dos, por favor.**

The menu, please. **La carta, por favor.**

What do you recommend? **¿Qué nos recomienda?**

We will begin with salad. **Empezaremos con ensalada.**

How long will it take? **¿Cuánto tiempo tomará?**

A cup of black coffee, please. **Un café solo, por favor.**

Do you have any cold drinks? **¿Tiene bebidas frías?**

Bring me a beer. **Tráigame una cerveza.**

How is the soup tonight? **¿Qué tal está la sopa esta noche?**

Could you bring us some more water? **¿Nos puede traer más agua?**

I want to pay the bill. **Quiero pagar la cuenta.**

We're in a hurry. **Tenemos prisa.**

Does that include service and tax? **¿Incluye servicio e impuestos?**

Keep the change. **Quédese con el cambio.**

In Need of Assistance

Help! **¡Socorro! ¡Emergencia!**

Please help me. **Favor de ayudarme.**

Can I use the telephone, please? **¿Puedo usar el teléfono, por favor?**

I feel sick. **Me siento mal.**

I have a stomachache. **Tengo dolor del estómago.**

I have high blood pressure. **Tengo la tensión alta.**

I have hurt my leg. **Me he hecho daño en la pierna.**

My husband is sick. **Mi esposo está enfermo.**

He has a fever. **Tiene fiebre.**

I need a doctor. **Necesito un médico.**

Is there a doctor here? **¿Hay un médico aquí?**

Can you give me a prescription for this? **¿Puede darme una receta para esto?**

Can you give me something for a stomachache? **¿Puede darme una cura para dolor de estómago?**

There has been an accident. **Ha habido un accidente.**

There is a fire. **Hay un incendio.**

Call the police. **Llame a la policía.**

Call an ambulance. **Llame a una ambulancia.**

Your name and address, please. **Su nombre y dirección, por favor.**

His license number was... **Su matrícula era...**

I am very sorry, officer. **Lo siento mucho, agente.**

I did not understand the sign. **No entendí el letrero.**

What is the speed limit? **¿Qué límite de velocidad hay?**

I want to see a lawyer. **Quiero ver a un abogado.**

**25
coe**

Fill it up, please. **Lleno, por favor.**

Check the water and oil. **Revíseme el agua y el aceite.**

Could you check the tires? **¿Podría revisar la presión de las llantas?**

There is something wrong with my car. **Mi coche no va bien.**

I have a flat tire. **Tengo una llanta pinchada.**

The battery is dead. **La batería está descargada.**

The engine is hot. **El motor está caliente.**

I need a new fan belt. **Necesito una correa de ventilador.**

Is there a gas station nearby? **¿Hay una estación de servicio cerca de aquí?**

Can you fix it? **¿Puede arreglarlo?**

How long will it take to fix it? **¿Cuánto tardará en repararlo?**

I need it urgently. **Lo necesito urgentemente.**

Idiomatic Uses of the Verb *Hacer*

hacer cola to stand in line

hacer escala to have a layover

hacer preguntas to ask questions

hacer un viaje to take a trip

hacer una fiesta to have a party

hacer(se) to become

Other Useful Terms and Phrases

a little **un poco**

a waste of time **una pérdida de tiempo**

a year ago **hace un año**

about, around **a eso de**

above all **sobre todo**

across, through **a través de**

again **otra vez**

against **en contra de**

all of a sudden **de repente**

all right **está bien**

alone, by oneself **a solas**

another time **otra vez**

anytime **a cualquier hora**

anyway **de todos modos**

25
coe

apparently **por lo visto**
around the corner **a la vuelta**
as far as **en cuanto a**
as for me **por mi parte**
as if **como si**
as soon as **en cuanto**
as soon as possible **cuanto antes**
ask a question (of) **hacer una pregunta (a)**
at dawn **al amanecer**
at every moment **a cada instante**
at first **al principio**
at home **en casa**
at last **al cabo**
at least **por lo menos**
at once **en seguida**
at the last minute **a última hora**
at the same time **al mismo tiempo**
at times, sometimes **a veces**
at your service **a sus órdenes**
baked **al horno**
be on a diet **estar a dieta**
businessman (woman) **hombre (mujer) de negocios**
by air mail **por avión**
by bicycle **en bicicleta**
by car **en coche**
by chance **por casualidad**
by day **de día**
by hand **a mano**
by heart **de memoria**
by leaps and bounds **a saltos**
by night **de noche**
by phone **por teléfono**
call attention to **llamar la atención**
call on the phone **llamar por teléfono**
consequently **por consiguiente**
credit card **tarjeta de crédito**

25
coe

each time **cada vez**

every day **todos los días**

everybody **todo el mundo**

everywhere **por todas partes**

finally, at last **por fin**

first of all **ante todo**

for certain, for sure **por cierto**

for example **por ejemplo**

for now **por ahora**

for that reason **por eso**

for the present **por ahora**

forever **para siempre**

frequently **con frecuencia**

from day to day **de día en día**

from now on **de aquí en adelante**

from time to time **de vez en cuando**

gain weight **aumentar(se) de peso**

generally **por lo general**

gladly **con mucho gusto**

have something to eat or drink **tomar algo**

if only **si ya**

in a bad mood **de mal humor**

in a few days **en pocos días**

in a hurry **de prisa**

in a little while **dentro de poco**

in a loud voice **en voz alta**

in a low voice **en voz baja**

in agreement **de acuerdo**

in and of itself **en sí**

in another way **de otra manera**

in case of **en caso de**

in fact **de hecho**

in fashion **de moda**

in front of **frente a**

in fun **en broma**

in good taste **de buen gusto**

in my opinion **a mi parecer**

in no way **de ninguna manera**

in place of **en lugar de**

in spite of **a pesar de**

in that way **de ese modo**

in the direction of **con rumbo a**

in the French style **a la francesa**

in the middle of **en medio de**

in the name of **en nombre de**

in this way **de esta manera**

in vain **en vano**

in writing **por escrito**

instead of **en vez de**

invite to one's house **invitar a casa**

just as it is **tal como es**

knock on the door **llamar a la puerta**

later **más tarde**

little by little **poco a poco**

lock **cerrar con llave**

look on to, to face **dar a**

lose weight **bajar de peso**

luckily **por suerte**

to mail **echar al correo**

make a stop **hacer escala**

many times **muchas veces**

maybe **tal vez**

to me, as far as I am concerned **para mí**

money order **giro postal**

more or less **más o menos**

nevertheless **sin embargo**

no longer **ya no**

not yet **todavía no**

nowadays **hoy día**

nowhere **en ninguna parte**

**25
coe**

often **a menudo**

on board **a bordo**

on foot **a pie**

on horseback **a caballo**

on the contrary **al contrario**

on the occasion of **con motivo de**

on the other hand **en cambio**

on the way to **camino a**

on time **a tiempo**

once **una vez**

once more **una vez más**

one of these days **un día de éstos**

otherwise **de otro modo**

out of style **pasado de moda**

outdoors **al aire libre**

pay attention to **hacer caso**

per day **por día**

per week **por semana**

presently **a poco**

rarely **pocas veces**

to ride a bicycle **dar un paseo en bicicleta**

right here **aquí mismo**

right now, right away **ahora mismo**

roommate **compañero de apartamento**

several times **varias veces**

to shake hands **dar la mano**

shortly after **poco después**

shortly before **poco antes**

to shout **dar voces**

sometime **alguna vez**

sometimes, at times **a veces**

standing **de pie**

step by step **paso a paso**

straighten one's room **arreglar el cuarto**

suddenly **de repente**

to sunbathe **tomar el sol**

to take a walk **dar un paseo**

talk on the phone **hablar por teléfono**

that very thing **eso mismo**

the bad part **lo malo**

the best part **lo mejor**

the good part **lo bueno**

the matter of **eso de**

the only thing **lo único**

the same **lo mismo**

therefore **por eso, por lo tanto**

this very day **hoy mismo**

this way **por aquí**

to welcome **dar la bienvenida**

unfortunately **por desgracia**

until later **hasta después**

until now **hasta ahora**

until then **hasta entonces**

up-to-date **al día**

wait in line **hacer cola**

whatever it may be **sea lo que sea**

willingly **de buena gana**

with regard to **en cuanto a**

with your permission **con permiso**

without a doubt **sin duda**

without fail **sin falta**

worth **por valor de**

**25
coe**

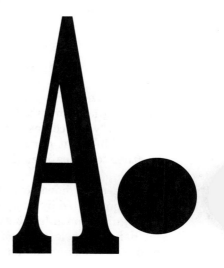

APPENDIX A

Glossary of English Grammar Terms

Students who have trouble learning Spanish often do not understand English very well. When writing or speaking English, they simply do "what comes naturally"—they have long forgotten the role that the different parts of speech play, the rules of syntax, and all the other technicalities that make language so "natural."

It is the case, however, that learning a second language can be greatly simplified by comparing it with the first and by understanding linguistic parallels between the two. The following list of terms and definitions is to remind English speakers of their linguistic building blocks and to identify the associations between English and Spanish. Since the focus here is on the English, most examples given are strictly the English illustrations, *except* when there is a significant difference in Spanish usage or when the concept is unique to Spanish.

Words appearing in definitions in SMALL CAPITAL LETTERS are themselves defined terms in the glossary and may be reviewed for further clarification or elaboration.

Active Voice — A construction in which the SUBJECT performs the action. *The boy ate the cherry pie.*

Adjective — A word used to MODIFY a NOUN. There are five basic types of adjectives: DESCRIPTIVE, DEMONSTRATIVE, INTERROGATIVE, LIMITING, and POSSESSIVE.

Adjective and Noun Agreement — In Spanish, INFLECTIONS of ADJECTIVES and NOUNS match to indicate GENDER and NUMBER. *yellow books* **libros amarillos**

Adjective Phrase — A PHRASE that serves as an ADJECTIVE. *The business, **twenty years old today**, still prospers.*

Adjective Series — Two or more ADJECTIVES modifying the same NOUN or nouns. *The **beautiful, rich,** and **gentle** man.*

Adverb — A word used to MODIFY a VERB, ADJECTIVE, or other adverb. Adverbs generally answer the questions *when, where,* or *how.* *He walked **slowly** to the train.*

Adverb Series — Two or more ADVERBS in a series. *He talked **brightly** and **briskly**.*

Affirmative Sentence — A SENTENCE that is not negative and that is not in a question or COMMAND form. *She rides her bike expertly.*

Affix — A word or part of a word added to another to inflect its meaning. See **Prefix** and **Suffix**.

Agreement — A condition whereby different parts of speech in a sentence must correspond syntactically. In English, the most common forms of agreement are between SUBJECT and VERB and between PRONOUN and ANTECEDENT. In Spanish, there is also frequent need for agreement between ADJECTIVE and NOUN and between ARTICLE and NOUN. See specific examples.

Antecedent — The NOUN or noun phrase referred to by a PRONOUN. *The **baby** is crying. **She** needs to be fed.* See also **Referent**.

Article — A word that precedes a NOUN to indicate its state of definiteness. *I threw **the** ball.*

Article and Noun Agreement — In Spanish, INFLECTIONS of ARTICLES and NOUNS match to indicate GENDER and NUMBER. *the books **los libros**, the flower **la flor***

Augmentative — A word or AFFIX that indicates a large size. *a **grand** celebration*

Auxiliary Verb — A VERB that combines with a CONJUGATED form of another VERB to convey the full TENSE of the VERB PHRASE. *They **have** traveled through Columbia frequently.*

Clause — A group of words that includes at least a SUBJECT and a VERB and forms a SENTENCE or part of a SENTENCE. *The school, **which is well known**, ...*

Cognate — A word related to another by descent from the same linguistic origin. They are often similar in spelling and meaning. *University **Universidad***

Collective Noun — A singular NOUN that signifies a group of persons or things. *The **choir** rose to sing.*

A

Command — A command is an IMPERATIVE SENTENCE. It is used to give an order. *Go to the store right away.*

Common Noun — A NOUN signifying a thing in general. *The mountain looked magnificent.*

Comparative — A language form of ADJECTIVES and ADVERBS used to compare two or more things. *My car is **faster** than yours.*

Comparative Adjective — An ADJECTIVE in a COMPARATIVE. *Ellen is **taller** than Mary.*

Compound Noun — A NOUN made up of two or more words. *Give me a **rubber band**.*

Compound Tense or Compound Verb — Any VERB TENSE that is made up of two or more words. *The children **are running** to the store.*

Conditional Perfect Tense — A PERFECT TENSE used to express an action that would have occurred if something else did not happen. *The boys **would have stopped** if they knew it was wrong.*

Conditional Tense — A verb TENSE used to express an action or event that would occur. *If she had time, she **would visit** the museum.*

Conjugation — The structure of inflectional verb forms required to express a VERB in all of its TENSES and MOODS and for all PERSONS and NUMBER combinations.

Conjugated Verb — A specific verb inflection expressing a VERB in a particular TENSE and MOOD. *He **saw** the accident.*

Conjunction — A part of speech that connects words, PHRASES, CLAUSES, or SENTENCES. *the girl **and** her doll*

Consonant — Any letter of the alphabet whose pronunciation involves closure of the vocal channel. Any letter that is *not* **a, e, i, o, u,** or **y.**

Contraction — A shortening of a combination of words. *He will not.* → *He **won't**.* In Spanish, there are only two contractions: **al** (**a** + **el**) and **del** (**de** + **el**).

Declarative Sentence — A SENTENCE that makes an AFFIRMATIVE or NEGATIVE statement. *Birds sing in the early morning.*

Definite Article — An ARTICLE that indicates a particular, definite NOUN. *They rode in the car.*

Demonstrative — A word that modifies a NOUN or VERB by distinguishing it from another of the same class. *Give me that book.*

Demonstrative Adjective — An ADJECTIVE that modifies a NOUN by distinguishing it from another. *I love those songs.*

Demonstrative Adverb — An ADVERB that modifies a VERB by distinguishing it from another. *Take me there.*

Demonstrative Pronoun — A PRONOUN that replaces a NOUN previously identified. *Call in the remaining men—those in the field.*

Dependent (Subordinate) Clause — A CLAUSE that, by itself, is not a complete SENTENCE and thus does not convey complete meaning. *While they were standing there, the accident occurred.*

Descriptive Adjective — An ADJECTIVE that indicates quality or condition. *a gloomy night*

Diminutive — A word or AFFIX that indicates small size. *cigarette*

Diphthong — Two adjacent VOWELS that are pronounced as one SYLLABLE. *I have no doubt.* In Spanish, at least one of the two VOWELS must be "weak" (**u, i,** or **y**): **traigo** *(I bring).* Two strong VOWELS together are termed an hiatus, and the vowels are pronounced as two SYLLABLES: **traer** *(to bring).*

Direct Command — An IMPERATIVE SENTENCE, in which an order is given and meant for the SUBJECT. *Finish your dinner.*

Direct Object — A NOUN or PRONOUN that receives the action of the VERB. A direct object generally answers the questions *what* or *whom. She kicked the ball.*

Exclamatory Sentence or Exclamation — A SENTENCE indicating strong feelings or expressed with great emphasis. Exclamation points are used in punctuation. *This is an outrage!*

Familiar Second Person — The SECOND PERSON used in Spanish with informal speech, when the "you" is someone younger than the speaker or someone whom the speaker knows well.

Feminine Gender — One of two GENDER categories; the other is MASCULINE. In Spanish, every NOUN has GENDER, and it is expected that all associated ARTICLES, ADJECTIVES, and PRONOUNS will be in AGREEMENT with the NOUN.

First Person — PRONOUN and VERB inflections that refer to the speaker or writer *(I, we)*. *I exercise every day.*

Formal Second Person — The SECOND PERSON **usted** and **ustedes** are used in Spanish in formal speech, when the "you" is someone to whom respect should be shown.

Future Perfect Tense — A PERFECT TENSE used to express a future action or an event completed before another future action or event. *After this child, the woman will have given birth six times.*

Future Tense — A SIMPLE TENSE used to express an action or event that will occur in the future. *Our party candidate will win.*

Gender and **Gender Agreement** — In Spanish, all NOUNS are either MASCULINE or FEMININE and must be syntactically combined with the appropriate parts of speech that reflect this classification.

Gerund — A PRESENT PARTICIPLE (the *-ing* form of the VERB) used as a NOUN. In Spanish, the same idea is expressed with the INFINITIVE. *Seeing is believing.* **Ver es creer.**

Idiom — An expression whose meaning cannot be derived from the literal interpretation of the words. As such, an idiom is not easily translated into another language. *The young lovers wanted to paint the town red.*

Imperative Mood — The VERB form used to denote an order or a COMMAND. *Come here now.*

Imperative Sentence — A SENTENCE expressed in the IMPERATIVE MOOD—another name for a COMMAND. *Hand me my walking shoes.*

Imperfect Progressive Tense — See **Past Progressive Tense**.

Imperfect Tense — One of two simple PAST TENSES in Spanish (the other is the PRETERITE). It is used to express actions that occurred in the past with no specific beginning or end. *My family always **traveled** in the summer.*

Indefinite Article — An ARTICLE that indicates an unspecified person or object. *I see **a** house.*

Indefinite Pronoun — A PRONOUN that does *not* refer to a specific person, to a specific time, or to a clearly defined condition. *any, something, no one*

Independent (Main) Clause — A CLAUSE that conveys complete meaning and can stand by itself. ***The man left the house** before the party was over.*

Indicative Mood — The VERB form used to indicate a statement of fact. It is the most common of the three MOODS. *The horse **runs** into the barn when it rains.*

Indirect Command — An IMPERATIVE SENTENCE in which the COMMAND meant for one person is relayed to another. *Have her come home now.*

Indirect Object — A NOUN or PRONOUN that receives the action of the VERB indirectly. An indirect object generally answers the questions *to what* or *to whom*. *The man gave (to) the **girl** a ring.*

Infinitive — The uninflected form of a VERB, indicating no SUBJECT or NUMBER. English infinitives include the word *to*. Spanish infinitives are one word, ending either in **-ar**, **-er**, or **-ir**. *to fly* **volar**

Inflection — Form of a word indicating GENDER, NUMBER, PERSON, VOICE, TENSE and/or MOOD.

Interrogative Adjective — An ADJECTIVE that introduces a question. ***What** ship is still at sea?*

Interrogative Adverb — An ADVERB used to introduce a question. ***Where** are we going?*

Interrogative Pronoun — A PRONOUN used to introduce a question. ***Who** is crying now?*

Interrogative Sentence — A SENTENCE that asks a question. *Why do birds sing?*

Intransitive Verb — A VERB that does not convey an action and does not require a DIRECT OBJECT. *The lion **sleeps**.*

Irregular Verb — A VERB that does not follow a standard set of CONJUGATION rules.

Limiting Adjective — An ADJECTIVE that describes the size or quantity of a NOUN or PRONOUN. *There are **many** ways to tell a story.*

Main Clause — See **Independent Clause**.

Masculine Gender — One of two GENDER categories; the other is FEMININE. In Spanish, every NOUN has GENDER, and it is expected that all associated ARTICLES, ADJECTIVES, and PRONOUNS will be in AGREEMENT with the NOUN.

Modify — An effect of an ADJECTIVE or ADVERB in clarifying or explaining the word it accompanies. ***large** house*

Mood — Inflectional forms that reflect the certainty or strength of the VERB. There are three different moods in English and Spanish: INDICATIVE, SUBJUNCTIVE, and IMPERATIVE.

Near Future Condition — A VERB form that indicates something about to happen. *We are **going** to the movies.*

Negative Sentence — A SENTENCE that includes a negation. *He does **not** know how to ride a bike.*

Neuter Demonstrative Pronoun — A PRONOUN used to point out something that is unspecified or unidentified. *What was **that**?*

Nominalized Adjective — An ADJECTIVE that is used as a NOUN. In English, the word *one* or *ones* is usually stated or implied. *I want the **red one**.* In Spanish, the ADJECTIVE stands with the ARTICLE. **Quiero el rojo.**

Noun — A word that signifies a person, animal, place, thing, event, idea, or quality.

Noun Series — A string of two or more nouns in a SENTENCE. *Give the children **cereal**, **bread**, and **sausage**.*

Number — Inflectional forms that indicate singularity or plurality.

Number Adjective — See **Ordinal**.

Number Agreement — A condition requiring that the form of a NOUN agree in number with a VERB and/or that the form of an ARTICLE, ADJECTIVE, or PRONOUN agree in number with the NOUN it refers to, attends, or modifies. *The rivers flow*.

Object — A NOUN or PRONOUN (or PHRASE that serves as either) that receives an action or follows a PREPOSITION. *She drove the car*.

Object Pronoun — A pronoun that receives an action or is the object of a PREPOSITION. In Spanish, there are different pronoun forms depending on the type of object involved. *The band played for us*.

Ordinal (Number Adjective) — The form of a number indicating position in a sequence. *He was the third batter*.

Participle — A VERB form used in combination with an AUXILIARY VERB to form a TENSE. It can also be used as an ADJECTIVE or ADVERB. See PAST and PRESENT PARTICIPLES.

Passive Voice — A construction in which the SUBJECT receives the action of a VERB. *The cherry pie was eaten by the boy*.

Past Participle — A PARTICIPLE that suggests completion. It is used as an ADJECTIVE or with an AUXILIARY VERB to form a PERFECT TENSE or the PASSIVE VOICE. *The game has started*.

Past Perfect (Pluperfect) Tense — A PERFECT TENSE used to express an action completed before another. *They left before the fire began*.

Past Progressive Tense — A COMPOUND TENSE that expresses actions in progress in the past. *The snow was falling*.

Past Tense — Any one of several verb TENSES used to express actions that occurred in the past. *Last week, he left school*.

Perfect Tense — A COMPOUND TENSE made up of an INFLECTION of the AUXILIARY VERB *to have* (**haber**) and a PAST PARTICIPLE. *I have never seen a house so beautiful*.

A

Person — The forms of PRONOUNS or VERBS that indicate either the one speaking *(I, we)*, the one spoken to *(you)*, or the one spoken about *(he, she, it, they)*.

Personified Noun — A non-human NOUN to which human qualities are attributed. *The **tree** cried for love.*

Phrase — A group of two or more related words that does not contain both a SUBJECT and a VERB. Phrases commonly begin with PREPOSITIONS. *I went **to the beach**.*

Pluperfect Tense — See **Past Perfect Tense**.

Plural — A condition indicating more than one person or thing. *There are many **problems** in the city.*

Possessive Adjective — An ADJECTIVE used to indicate ownership. ***my** coffee **Dad's** pipe*

Possessive Phrase — A PHRASE that indicates ownership. *That friend **of mine** is always getting into trouble.*

Possessive Pronoun — A PRONOUN used to indicate ownership. *The victory was **his**.*

Predicate — The part of a SENTENCE that contains the VERB or VERB PHRASE and expresses the action of the SENTENCE or what is said of the SUBJECT. *The soccer game **ended in a tie**.*

Prefix — A word or part of a word added to the beginning of a base to create a derivative word. ***pre**certification*

Preposition — A word that shows the relationship of a NOUN or PRONOUN to another word in the SENTENCE. *She was given the keys **to** the city.*

Prepositional Phrase — The group of words made up of a preposition, its OBJECT, and any related modifiers. *They met **in the rose garden**.*

Present Participle — A PARTICIPLE that suggests an ongoing action. It can be used with an AUXILIARY verb to form a PROGRESSIVE TENSE, or it can be used as an ADJECTIVE.

Present Perfect Tense — A PERFECT TENSE used to express a completed action without reference to a specific time. *She **has gone** to the store.*

Present Progressive Tense — A COMPOUND TENSE that expresses actions in progress in the present. *The sun **is shining**.*

Present Tense — Any one of several verb tenses used to express actions occurring at the present time. *I now **pronounce** you man and wife.*

Preterite Tense — One of two simple PAST TENSES in Spanish (the other is the IMPERFECT). It is used to express past actions that were completed at a specific time. *The actors **walked** on stage.*

Progressive Tense — A COMPOUND TENSE made up of an INFLECTION of the VERB *to be* (**estar**) and a PRESENT PARTICIPLE. See **Present Progressive** and **Past Progressive**.

Pronoun — A word that takes the place of a NOUN. ***They** gave **her** an award.*

Pronoun and Noun Agreement — In English and Spanish, INFLECTIONS of PRONOUNS and their ANTECEDENTS match to indicate GENDER, NUMBER, and PERSON. *The **girl** walked in, and **she** saw **her** friend.* **La muchacha entró, y ella vio a su amiga.**

Proper Noun — A NOUN that denotes a specific thing and is usually capitalized in English. *The **Sierras** are magnificent.*

Recent Past Condition — A construction using a VERB PHRASE to indicate something that has just happened. *The class **has just** turned in the final exam.*

Reciprocal Pronoun — A PRONOUN used to indicate a plural subject involved in mutual action or in a cross-relationship. *They patted **each other** on the back.*

Referent — A NOUN or noun phrase to which a PRONOUN refers. *The **student** spoke in his class...* See also **Antecedent**.

Reflexive Pronoun — A PRONOUN that has the same identity as the SUBJECT to which it refers. *I shot **myself** in the foot.*

Reflexive Verb — A VERB of which the object is the same as the subject. The REFLEXIVE PRONOUN is always used with reflexive verbs. *He **washed** himself.*

Regular Verb — A VERB that follows a set of standard CONJUGATION rules.

Relative Adjective — An ADJECTIVE that introduces a DEPENDENT CLAUSE. *The doctor, **whose** patient this is, expressed concern.*

Relative Pronoun — A PRONOUN that introduces a DEPENDENT CLAUSE. Its ANTECEDENT is usually identified. *They caught the man **who** did it.*

Root (or Stem) — In Spanish, the part of a VERB that results from dropping the last two letters of the INFINITIVE: **hablar** → **habl-**

Second Person — PRONOUN and VERB inflections that refer to the person being spoken to. ***You need** to get better grades.*

Sentence — A syntactically related group of words that expresses a complete thought. There are four types of sentences: DECLARATIVE, INTERROGATIVE, IMPERATIVE, and EXCLAMATORY. Sentences can also be AFFIRMATIVE or NEGATIVE.

Simple Tense — Any verb TENSE made up of a single word. *The dog **barked** loudly.*

Singular — A condition indicating one person or thing. *The **story** of man is still being told.*

Soft Command — A gentle form of COMMAND, usually expressed in the context of an action that is expected or desired. *I wish that he would leave that job.*

Statement — See **Declarative Sentence**.

Stem — See **Root**.

Stem-Changing Verb — Any Spanish VERB whose ROOT spelling changes according to its CONJUGATION.

Stress — The vocal emphasis placed on a SYLLABLE or a word to indicate relative prominence in pronunciation.

Subject — The word or group of words predicated in a SENTENCE. The subject can perform or receive the action. *The shy student gave an outstanding book report. An outstanding book report was given by the shy student.*

Subject and Verb Agreement — In English and Spanish, INFLECTIONS of SUBJECTS and VERBS match to indicate NUMBER. *The students are coming back. Los estudiantes regresan.*

Subject Pronoun — A PRONOUN that serves as the subject of a SENTENCE. *We need to eat.*

A

Subjunctive Mood — The mode of a VERB used to express subjectivity and uncertainty. This is much more prevalent in Spanish than English. *I wish I were the queen of England.*

Subordinate Clause — See **Dependent Clause**.

Suffix — A word or part of a word added to the end of a base to create a derivative word. *successful*

Suggestion Command — A gentle form of COMMAND that is presented as a suggestion. *Let's go to the beach.*

Superlative — The form of ADJECTIVES and ADVERBS used to establish the extreme. *He is the best student in the class.*

Syllable — A unit of spoken language consisting of one or more vowel sounds alone or followed by or preceded by a consonant sound. A word is made up of one or more syllables.

Tense — The VERB inflection that indicates when the action takes place: PAST, PRESENT, or FUTURE.

Third Person — PRONOUN or VERB inflections that refer to the person or thing being spoken about. *They train for hours in the morning.*

Transitive Verb — A VERB that conveys an action. Such verbs require DIRECT OBJECTS. *The little girl touched the rabbit.*

Verb — A word that expresses an action, event, condition, or state of being. *Rain fell from the sky.*

Verb Phrase — A PHRASE that works as a VERB to convey TENSE. *She* ***has been crying*** *about school.*

Voice — A distinction applied to a SENTENCE to indicate the relationship between the SUBJECT and its VERB. See **Active Voice** and **Passive Voice**.

Vowel — Any letter of the alphabet whose pronunciation is open—does not involve a closure or constriction of the vocal channel. The following letters are vowels in English and Spanish: **a**, **e**, **i**, **o**, **u**, **y**.

A

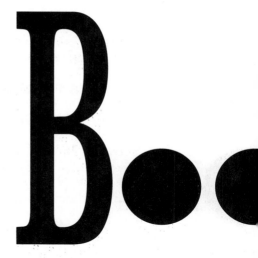

Glossary of Commonly Confused and Misused Terms

to appear:	**parecer, aparecer**, and **asomar(se)**
to ask:	**pedir** and **preguntar**
to become:	**llegar a ser, poner(se), hacer(se), volver(se)**
to be:	**ser** and **estar** (page 86)
but:	**pero** and **sino (que)** (page 45)
country:	**campo, nación, país**, and **patria**
for:	**para** and **por** (page 49)
to give:	**dar**
to go:	**andar, ir**, and **ir(se)**
to have:	**tener** and **haber** (page 88)
here:	**aquí** and **acá**
to know:	**saber** and **conocer**
to leave:	**dejar** and **salir**
little:	**poco** and **pequeño**
obligation:	**deber, deber de**, and **tener que**
to play:	**jugar** and **tocar**
to remember:	**acordar(se)** and **recordar**
to return:	**volver, regresar, devolver**
to spend:	**gastar** and **pasar**
to take:	**llevar** and **tomar**
there:	**ahí, allí**, and **allá**
to think:	**pensar**
very much:	**muy** and **mucho**
what, who, which:	**que, cual**, and **quien** (page 41)

B

TO APPEAR: **PARECER, APARECER**, AND **ASOMAR(SE)**

Parecer means *to appear* as in *to seem*.

Parecen contentos en la escuela nueva.
They *appear* happy in the new school.

Aparecer and **asomar(se)** both mean *to appear; to show up.*

Los niños corrieron cuando el hombre *apareció*.
The children ran when the man *appeared*.

Él *se asomó* sin aviso.
He *appeared* without warning.

TO ASK: **PEDIR** AND **PREGUNTAR**

Pedir means *to ask for something, to request.*

La estudiante le *pidió* ayuda al profesor.
The student *asked* the professor *for* help.

Preguntar means *to ask a question, to inquire.*

El médico le *preguntó* al niño cómo estaba.
The doctor *asked* the boy how he was.

TO BECOME: **LLEGAR A SER, PONER(SE), HACER(SE), VOLVER(SE)**

Llegar a ser means *to become,* as in attaining a goal after considerable effort.

Yo *llegaré a ser* novelista.
I *will become* a novelist.

Poner(se) expresses *to become* with most descriptive adjectives.

Ellos *se pusieron* muy tristes.
They *became* very sad.

Hacer(se), literally meaning *to make oneself,* is used with professions, religious and political affiliations, and other descriptive adjectives.

Ella *se hacía* una mujer rica.
She *became* a rich woman.

Volver(se) expresses *to become something unexpected* such as *crazy* (**loco**).

El cura *se volvió loco.*
The priest *became crazy*.

B

TO BE: **SER** AND **ESTAR** (PAGE 86)

BUT: **PERO** AND **SINO (QUE)** (PAGE 45)

COUNTRY: **CAMPO**, **PAÍS**, **PATRIA**, AND **NACIÓN**

Campo means *country,* as in *countryside.*

Viven en el *campo* ahora.
Now they live in the *country*.

País means *country,* as in *nation* or *geographic region.*

¿Qué *país* es tu favorito?
What *country* is your favorite?

Nación means *country,* as in *nation.*

Las dos *naciones* están en paz.
The two *countries* are at peace.

Patria means *country,* as in *native land.*

¿Regresará a su *patria* pronto?
Will you return to your *country* soon?

FOR: **PARA** AND **POR** (PAGE 49)

TO GIVE: **DAR**

Dar *to give*

Te *doy* mi corazón.
I *give* you my heart.

Dar a *to face*

Nosotros *damos a* problemas nuevos cada día.
We *face* new problems each day.

Dar con *to meet, to come upon*

Yo *di con* una gran idea.
I *came upon* a great notion.

Dar en *to hit, to land*

El barco *dio en* suelo ayer.
The boat *landed* yesterday.

TO GO: **ANDAR**, **IR**, AND **IR(SE)**

Andar means *to go,* when the subject is an animal or an inanimate object.

Su coche no *anda*.
His car does not *go*.

Ir means *to go to a destination*.

***Iremos* a la playa mañana.**
We will go to the beach tomorrow.

Ir(se) means *to go away*.

¡Váyase, por favor!
Go away, please!

TO HAVE: **TENER** AND **HABER** (PAGE 88)

HERE: **AQUÍ** AND **ACÁ**

Aquí means *here,* a location close to the speaker.

Yo visité *aquí* la semana pasada.
I visited *here* last week.

Acá means *here,* when used with a verb of motion.

Mi amiga maneja *acá.*
My friend is driving *here.*

B

TO KNOW: **SABER** AND **CONOCER**

Saber means *to know facts* and *to know how (to)* when followed by an infinitive. In the preterite tense, it means *to find out.*

Nosotros *sabemos* nadar.
We *know how* to swim.

Conocer means *to be familiar or acquainted with.* In the preterite tense, it means *to meet.*

***Conozco* la ciudad de París.**
I *know* Paris.
***Conocí* a tu hermana ayer por la primera vez.**
I *met* your sister yesterday for the first time.

TO LEAVE: **DEJAR** AND **SALIR**

Dejar means *to leave behind.*

Yo *dejaré* mis llaves.
I *will leave* my keys.

Salir means *to leave* as in *to go out.*

Él *salió de* la fiesta.
He *left* the party.

LITTLE: **POCO** AND **PEQUEÑO**

Poco means *little* in terms of quantity.

Tengo *poco* dinero.
I have *little* money.

Pequeño means *little* in terms of size.

Viven en una casa *pequeña*.
They live in a *small* house.

B

OBLIGATION: **DEBER**, **DEBER DE**, AND **TENER QUE**

Deber means *ought to,* as in a moral obligation.

***Debo* trabajar ahora.**
I *ought* to work now.

Deber de means *must be,* as in a probable situation.

La profesora *debe de* estar en la oficina.
The professor *must be* in the office.

Tener que means *must,* as in to have to do something.

***Tengo que* dormir ahora.**
I *have to* sleep now.

TO PLAY: **JUGAR** AND **TOCAR**

Jugar means *to play a game.*

Ella *juega* muy bien al fútbol.
She *plays* soccer very well.

Tocar means *to play* a musical instrument.

Quiero *tocar* el piano.
I want *to play* the piano.

TO REMEMBER: **ACORDAR(SE)** AND **RECORDAR**

Acordar(se) means *to remember.*

Lo siento, pero no *me acuerdo* de su nombre.
I'm sorry, but I don't *remember* your name.

Recordar means *to remind* or *to recall.*

Lo siento, pero no recuerdo su nombre.
I'm sorry, but I do not *recall* your name.

Me *recuerda* de tu padre.
He *reminds* me of your father.

TO RETURN: **VOLVER, REGRESAR, DEVOLVER**

Volver and **regresar** mean *to return* as in *to come back.*

Quiero *volver* a casa.
I want *to return* to the house.

Regresará en la mañana.
He *will return* in the morning.

Devolver means *to return* as in *to give back.*

Necesito *devolver* los discos.
I need *to return* the records.

TO SPEND: **GASTAR** AND **PASAR**

Gastar means *to spend money.*

No *gasten* todo su dinero en la tienda.
Don't *spend* all your money at the store.

Pasar means *to spend time.*

Pasarán una semana en ese proyecto.
They *will spend* one week on that project.

TO TAKE: **LLEVAR** AND **TOMAR**

Llevar means *to carry* or *to transport*.

La mujer no *llevó* la ropa a la lavandería.
The woman did not *take* the clothes to the laundromat.

Tomar means *to take* or *to catch*.

***Tomamos* el último autobús.**
We *took* the last bus.

THERE: **AHÍ**, **ALLÍ**, AND **ALLÁ**

Ahí means *there,* close to the speaker.

Está *ahí*.
It is right *there*.

Allí means *there,* farther away from the speaker.

Póngalo *allí*.
Put it over *there*.

Allá means *there,* when used with a verb of motion.

Nadó *allá*.
He swam *there*.

TO THINK: **PENSAR**

Pensar means *to believe* or *to plan*.

Ella *piensa* regresar a su pueblo.
She *plans* to go back to her town.

Pensar en means *to think about*.

Pienso en dinero todos los días.
I *think about* money every day.

VERY, MUCH: **MUY** AND **MUCHO**

Muy is an adverb that means *very*.

Estuvo *muy* triste.
It was *very* sad.

Mucho is an adjective that means *much, many, a lot*.

Tengo *mucho* dinero.
I have *much* money.

B

The combination of **muy mucho** is incorrect in Spanish. **Muchísimo** is an expression equivalent to the English phrase *very much*.

WHO, WHICH: **QUE, CUAL**, AND **QUIEN (PAGE 41)**

Conjugations of Thirty Common Verbs

buscar to look for
comer to eat *(regular -er)*
conocer to know
construir to construct
corregir to correct
dar to give
decir to tell
dormir to sleep
empezar to begin
estar to be
haber to have *(auxiliary)*
hablar to speak *(regular -ar)*
hacer to do, make
ir(se) to go (away)
jugar to play

leer to read
mostrar to show
pedir to ask for
pensar to think
poder to be able
poner to put, place
querer to want, love
saber to know
salir to leave
ser to be
tener to have
traer to bring
venir to come
ver to see
vivir to live *(regular -ir)*

BUSCAR TO LOOK FOR

		Singular	*Plural*
Present **Indicative**	1st Person	**busco**	**buscamos**
	2nd Person *(fam.)*	**buscas**	**buscáis**[1]
	3rd Person, 2nd *(form.)*	**busca**	**buscan**
Present **Subjunctive**	1st Person	**busque**	**busquemos**
	2nd Person *(fam.)*	**busques**	**busquéis**
	3rd Person, 2nd *(form.)*	**busque**	**busquen**
Preterite	1st Person	**busqué**	**buscamos**
	2nd Person *(fam.)*	**buscaste**	**buscasteis**
	3rd Person, 2nd *(form.)*	**buscó**	**buscaron**
Imperfect **Indicative**	1st Person	**buscaba**	**buscábamos**
	2nd Person *(fam.)*	**buscabas**	**buscabais**
	3rd Person, 2nd *(form.)*	**buscaba**	**buscaban**
Imperfect **Subjunctive**	1st Person	**buscara**	**buscáramos**
	2nd Person *(fam.)*	**buscaras**	**buscarais**
	3rd Person, 2nd *(form.)*	**buscara**	**buscaran**
Future	1st Person	**buscaré**	**buscaremos**
	2nd Person *(fam.)*	**buscarás**	**buscaréis**
	3rd Person, 2nd *(form.)*	**buscará**	**buscarán**
Conditional	1st Person	**buscaría**	**buscaríamos**
	2nd Person *(fam.)*	**buscarías**	**buscaríais**
	3rd Person, 2nd *(form.)*	**buscaría**	**buscarían**

Imperative	*Singular*	*Negative*	*Plural*
Formal Command	**busque**	**no busque**	} **busquen**
Familiar Command	**busca**	**no busques**	
Present Participle	**buscando**		
Past Participle	**buscado**		

---

[1] The second person familiar or **vosotros** form is a vestige of old Castillian. Today it is used only in Spain and in highly formal speech in Latin America.

COMER TO EAT *(REGULAR -ER)*

		Singular	*Plural*
Present	1st Person	**como**	**comemos**
Indicative	2nd Person *(fam.)*	**comes**	**coméis**
	3rd Person, 2nd *(form.)*	**come**	**comen**
Present	1st Person	**coma**	**comamos**
Subjunctive	2nd Person *(fam.)*	**comas**	**comáis**
	3rd Person, 2nd *(form.)*	**coma**	**coman**
Preterite	1st Person	**comí**	**comimos**
	2nd Person *(fam.)*	**comiste**	**comisteis**
	3rd Person, 2nd *(form.)*	**comió**	**comieran**
Imperfect	1st Person	**comía**	**comíamos**
Indicative	2nd Person *(fam.)*	**comías**	**comíais**
	3rd Person, 2nd *(form.)*	**comía**	**comían**
Imperfect	1st Person	**comiera**	**comiéramos**
Subjunctive	2nd Person *(fam.)*	**comieras**	**comierais**
	3rd Person, 2nd *(form.)*	**comiera**	**comieran**
Future	1st Person	**comeré**	**comeremos**
	2nd Person *(fam.)*	**comerás**	**comeréis**
	3rd Person, 2nd *(form.)*	**comerá**	**comerán**
Conditional	1st Person	**comería**	**comeríamos**
	2nd Person *(fam.)*	**comerías**	**comeríais**
	3rd Person, 2nd *(form.)*	**comería**	**comerían**

Imperative	*Singular*	*Negative*	*Plural*
Formal Command	**coma**	**no coma**	} **coman**
Familiar Command	**come**	**no comas**	
Present Participle	**comiendo**		
Past Participle	**comido**		

CONOCER TO KNOW

		Singular	*Plural*
Present	1st Person	conozco	conocemos
Indicative	2nd Person *(fam.)*	conoces	conocéis
	3rd Person, 2nd *(form.)*	conoce	conocen
Present	1st Person	conozca	conozcamos
Subjunctive	2nd Person *(fam.)*	conozcas	conozcáis
	3rd Person, 2nd *(form.)*	conozca	conozcan
Preterite	1st Person	conocí	conocimos
	2nd Person *(fam.)*	conociste	conocisteis
	3rd Person, 2nd *(form.)*	conoció	conocieron
Imperfect	1st Person	conocía	conocíamos
Indicative	2nd Person *(fam.)*	conocías	conocíais
	3rd Person, 2nd *(form.)*	conocía	conocían
Imperfect	1st Person	conociera	conociéramos
Subjunctive	2nd Person *(fam.)*	conocieras	conocierais
	3rd Person, 2nd *(form.)*	conociera	conocieran
Future	1st Person	conoceré	conoceremos
	2nd Person *(fam.)*	conocerás	conoceréis
	3rd Person, 2nd *(form.)*	conocerá	conocerán
Conditional	1st Person	conocería	conoceríamos
	2nd Person *(fam.)*	conocerías	conoceríais
	3rd Person, 2nd *(form.)*	conocería	conocerían

Imperative	*Singular*	*Negative*	*Plural*
Formal Command	conozca	no conozca	} conozcan
Familiar Command	conoce	no conozcas	
Present Participle	conociendo		
Past Participle	conocido		

CONSTRUIR TO CONSTRUCT

		Singular	*Plural*
Present	1st Person	construyo	construimos
Indicative	2nd Person *(fam.)*	construyes	construyís
	3rd Person, 2nd *(form.)*	construye	construyen
Present	1st Person	construya	construyamos
Subjunctive	2nd Person *(fam.)*	construyas	construyáis
	3rd Person, 2nd *(form.)*	construya	construyan
Preterite	1st Person	construí	construimos
	2nd Person *(fam.)*	construiste	construisteis
	3rd Person, 2nd *(form.)*	construyó	construyeron
Imperfect	1st Person	construía	construíamos
Indicative	2nd Person *(fam.)*	construías	construíais
	3rd Person, 2nd *(form.)*	construía	construían
Imperfect	1st Person	construyera	construyéramos
Subjunctive	2nd Person *(fam.)*	construyeras	construyerais
	3rd Person, 2nd *(form.)*	construyera	construyeran
Future	1st Person	construiré	construiremos
	2nd Person *(fam.)*	construirás	construiréis
	3rd Person, 2nd *(form.)*	construirá	construirán
Conditional	1st Person	construiría	construiríamos
	2nd Person *(fam.)*	construirías	construiríais
	3rd Person, 2nd *(form.)*	construiría	construirían

Imperative	*Singular*	*Negative*	*Plural*
Formal Command	construya	no construya	} construyan
Familiar Command	construye	no construyas	
Present Participle	construyendo		
Past Participle	construido		

CORREGIR TO CORRECT

		Singular	*Plural*
Present	1st Person	**corrijo**	**corregimos**
Indicative	2nd Person *(fam.)*	**corriges**	**corregís**
	3rd Person, 2nd *(form.)*	**corrige**	**corrigen**
Present	1st Person	**corrija**	**corrijamos**
Subjunctive	2nd Person *(fam.)*	**corrijas**	**corrijáis**
	3rd Person, 2nd *(form.)*	**corrija**	**corrijan**
Preterite	1st Person	**corregí**	**corregimos**
	2nd Person *(fam.)*	**corregiste**	**corregisteis**
	3rd Person, 2nd *(form.)*	**corrigió**	**corrigieron**
Imperfect	1st Person	**corregía**	**corregíamos**
Indicative	2nd Person *(fam.)*	**corregías**	**corregíais**
	3rd Person, 2nd *(form.)*	**corregía**	**corregían**
Imperfect	1st Person	**corrigiera**	**corrigiéramos**
Subjunctive	2nd Person *(fam.)*	**corrigieras**	**corrigierais**
	3rd Person, 2nd *(form.)*	**corrigiera**	**corrigieran**
Future	1st Person	**corregiré**	**corregiremos**
	2nd Person *(fam.)*	**corregirás**	**corregiréis**
	3rd Person, 2nd *(form.)*	**corregirá**	**corregirán**
Conditional	1st Person	**corregiría**	**corregiríamos**
	2nd Person *(fam.)*	**corregirías**	**corregiríais**
	3rd Person, 2nd *(form.)*	**corregiría**	**corregirían**

Imperative	*Singular*	*Negative*	*Plural*
Formal Command	**corrija**	**no corrija**	} **corrijan**
Familiar Command	**corrige**	**no corrijas**	
Present Participle	**corrigiendo**		
Past Participle	**corregido**		

DAR TO GIVE

		Singular	Plural
Present	1st Person	doy	damos
Indicative	2nd Person *(fam.)*	das	dais
	3rd Person, 2nd *(form.)*	da	dan
Present	1st Person	dé	demos
Subjunctive	2nd Person *(fam.)*	des	deis
	3rd Person, 2nd *(form.)*	dé	den
Preterite	1st Person	di	dimos
	2nd Person *(fam.)*	diste	disteis
	3rd Person, 2nd *(form.)*	dio	dieron
Imperfect	1st Person	daba	dábamos
Indicative	2nd Person *(fam.)*	dabas	dabais
	3rd Person, 2nd *(form.)*	daba	daban
Imperfect	1st Person	diera	diéramos
Subjunctive	2nd Person *(fam.)*	dieras	dierais
	3rd Person, 2nd *(form.)*	diera	dieran
Future	1st Person	daré	daremos
	2nd Person *(fam.)*	darás	daréis
	3rd Person, 2nd *(form.)*	dará	darán
Conditional	1st Person	daría	daríamos
	2nd Person *(fam.)*	darías	daríais
	3rd Person, 2nd *(form.)*	daría	darían

Imperative	Singular	Negative	Plural
Formal Command	dé	no dé	} den
Familiar Command	da	no des	
Present Participle	dando		
Past Participle	dado		

DECIR TO TELL

		Singular	Plural
Present	1st Person	digo	decimos
Indicative	2nd Person *(fam.)*	dices	decís
	3rd Person, 2nd *(form.)*	dice	dicen
Present	1st Person	diga	digamos
Subjunctive	2nd Person *(fam.)*	digas	digáis
	3rd Person, 2nd *(form.)*	diga	digan
Preterite	1st Person	dije	dijimos
	2nd Person *(fam.)*	dijiste	dijisteis
	3rd Person, 2nd *(form.)*	dijo	dijeron
Imperfect	1st Person	decía	decíamos
Indicative	2nd Person *(fam.)*	decías	decíais
	3rd Person, 2nd *(form.)*	decía	decían
Imperfect	1st Person	dijera	dijéramos
Subjunctive	2nd Person *(fam.)*	dijeras	dijerais
	3rd Person, 2nd *(form.)*	dijera	dijeran
Future	1st Person	diré	diremos
	2nd Person *(fam.)*	dirás	diréis
	3rd Person, 2nd *(form.)*	dirá	dirán
Conditional	1st Person	diría	diríamos
	2nd Person *(fam.)*	dirías	diríais
	3rd Person, 2nd *(form.)*	diría	dirían

Imperative	Singular	Negative	Plural
Formal Command	diga	no diga	} digan
Familiar Command	di	no digas	
Present Participle	diciendo		
Past Participle	dicho		

DORMIR TO SLEEP

		Singular	*Plural*
Present	1st Person	**duermo**	**dormimos**
Indicative	2nd Person *(fam.)*	**duermes**	**dormís**
	3rd Person, 2nd *(form.)*	**duerme**	**duermen**
Present	1st Person	**duerma**	**durmamos**
Subjunctive	2nd Person *(fam.)*	**duermas**	**durmáis**
	3rd Person, 2nd *(form.)*	**duerma**	**duerman**
Preterite	1st Person	**dormí**	**dormimos**
	2nd Person *(fam.)*	**dormiste**	**dormisteis**
	3rd Person, 2nd *(form.)*	**durmió**	**durmieron**
Imperfect	1st Person	**dormía**	**dormíamos**
Indicative	2nd Person *(fam.)*	**dormías**	**dormíais**
	3rd Person, 2nd *(form.)*	**dormía**	**dormían**
Imperfect	1st Person	**durmiera**	**durmiéramos**
Subjunctive	2nd Person *(fam.)*	**durmieras**	**durmierais**
	3rd Person, 2nd *(form.)*	**durmiera**	**durmieran**
Future	1st Person	**dormiré**	**dormiremos**
	2nd Person *(fam.)*	**dormirás**	**dormiréis**
	3rd Person, 2nd *(form.)*	**dormirá**	**dormirán**
Conditional	1st Person	**dormiría**	**dormiríamos**
	2nd Person *(fam.)*	**dormirías**	**dormiríais**
	3rd Person, 2nd *(form.)*	**dormiría**	**dormirían**

Imperative	*Singular*	*Negative*	*Plural*
Formal Command	**duerma**	**no duerma**	} **duerman**
Familiar Command	**duerme**	**no duermas**	

Present Participle	**durmiendo**
Past Participle	**dormido**

EMPEZAR TO BEGIN

		Singular	Plural
Present Indicative	1st Person	empiezo	empezamos
	2nd Person *(fam.)*	empiezas	empezáis
	3rd Person, 2nd *(form.)*	empieza	empiezan
Present Subjunctive	1st Person	empiece	empecemos
	2nd Person *(fam.)*	empieces	empecéis
	3rd Person, 2nd *(form.)*	empiece	empiecen
Preterite	1st Person	empecé	empezamos
	2nd Person *(fam.)*	empezaste	empezasteis
	3rd Person, 2nd *(form.)*	empezó	empezaron
Imperfect Indicative	1st Person	empezaba	empezábamos
	2nd Person *(fam.)*	empezabas	empezabais
	3rd Person, 2nd *(form.)*	empezaba	empezaban
Imperfect Subjunctive	1st Person	empezara	empezáramos
	2nd Person *(fam.)*	empezaras	empezarais
	3rd Person, 2nd *(form.)*	empezara	empezaran
Future	1st Person	empezaré	empezaremos
	2nd Person *(fam.)*	empezarás	empezaréis
	3rd Person, 2nd *(form.)*	empezará	empezarán
Conditional	1st Person	empezaría	empezaríamos
	2nd Person *(fam.)*	empezarías	empezaríais
	3rd Person, 2nd *(form.)*	empezaría	empezarían

Imperative	Singular	Negative	Plural
Formal Command	empiece	no empiece	} empiecen
Familiar Command	empieza	no empieces	
Present Participle	empezando		
Past Participle	empezado		

ESTAR TO BE

		Singular	*Plural*
Present	1st Person	estoy	estamos
Indicative	2nd Person *(fam.)*	estás	estáis
	3rd Person, 2nd *(form.)*	está	están
Present	1st Person	esté	estemos
Subjunctive	2nd Person *(fam.)*	estés	estéis
	3rd Person, 2nd *(form.)*	esté	estén
Preterite	1st Person	estuve	estuvimos
	2nd Person *(fam.)*	estuviste	estuvisteis
	3rd Person, 2nd *(form.)*	estuvo	estuvieron
Imperfect	1st Person	estaba	estábamos
Indicative	2nd Person *(fam.)*	estabas	estabais
	3rd Person, 2nd *(form.)*	estaba	estaban
Imperfect	1st Person	estuviera	estuviéramos
Subjunctive	2nd Person *(fam.)*	estuvieras	estuvierais
	3rd Person, 2nd *(form.)*	estuviera	estuvieron
Future	1st Person	estaré	estaremos
	2nd Person *(fam.)*	estarás	estaréis
	3rd Person, 2nd *(form.)*	estará	estarán
Conditional	1st Person	estaría	estaríamos
	2nd Person *(fam.)*	estarías	estaríais
	3rd Person, 2nd *(form.)*	estaría	estarían

Imperative	*Singular*	*Negative*	*Plural*
Formal Command	esté	no esté	} estén
Familiar Command	está	no estés	
Present Participle	estando		
Past Participle	estado		

HABER TO HAVE

Used only as an auxiliary verb (page 73)

		Singular	Plural
Present	1st Person	he	hemos
Indicative	2nd Person *(fam.)*	has	habéis
	3rd Person, 2nd *(form.)*	ha	han
Present	1st Person	haya	hayamos
Subjunctive	2nd Person *(fam.)*	hayas	hayáis
	3rd Person, 2nd *(form.)*	haya	hayan
Preterite	1st Person	hube	hubimos
	2nd Person *(fam.)*	hubiste	hubisteis
	3rd Person, 2nd *(form.)*	hubo	hubieron
Imperfect	1st Person	había	habíamos
Indicative	2nd Person *(fam.)*	habías	habíais
	3rd Person, 2nd *(form.)*	había	habían
Imperfect	1st Person	hubiera	hubiéramos
Subjunctive	2nd Person *(fam.)*	hubieras	hubierais
	3rd Person, 2nd *(form.)*	hubiera	hubieran
Future	1st Person	habré	habremos
	2nd Person *(fam.)*	habrás	habréis
	3rd Person, 2nd *(form.)*	habrá	habrán
Conditional	1st Person	habría	habríamos
	2nd Person *(fam.)*	habrías	habríais
	3rd Person, 2nd *(form.)*	habría	habrían

Imperative	Singular	Negative	Plural

Formal Command
$\Big\}$ (not applicable)
Familiar Command

Present Participle   habiendo

Past Participle   habido

HABLAR TO SPEAK *(REGULAR -AR)*

		Singular	*Plural*
Present	1st Person	hablo	hablamos
Indicative	2nd Person *(fam.)*	hablas	habláis
	3rd Person, 2nd *(form.)*	habla	hablan
Present	1st Person	hable	hablemos
Subjunctive	2nd Person *(fam.)*	hables	habléis
	3rd Person, 2nd *(form.)*	hable	hablen
Preterite	1st Person	hablé	hablamos
	2nd Person *(fam.)*	hablaste	hablasteis
	3rd Person, 2nd *(form.)*	habló	hablaron
Imperfect	1st Person	hablaba	hablábamos
Indicative	2nd Person *(fam.)*	hablabas	hablabais
	3rd Person, 2nd *(form.)*	hablaba	hablaban
Imperfect	1st Person	hablara	habláramos
Subjunctive	2nd Person *(fam.)*	hablaras	hablarais
	3rd Person, 2nd *(form.)*	hablara	hablaran
Future	1st Person	hablaré	hablaremos
	2nd Person *(fam.)*	hablarás	hablaréis
	3rd Person, 2nd *(form.)*	hablará	hablarán
Conditional	1st Person	hablaría	hablaríamos
	2nd Person *(fam.)*	hablarías	hablaríais
	3rd Person, 2nd *(form.)*	hablaría	hablarían

Imperative	*Singular*	*Negative*	*Plural*
Formal Command	hable	no hable	} hablen
Familiar Command	habla	no hables	

Present Participle	hablando
Past Participle	hablado

HACER TO DO, MAKE

		Singular	*Plural*
Present	1st Person	hago	hacemos
Indicative	2nd Person *(fam.)*	haces	hacéis
	3rd Person, 2nd *(form.)*	hace	hacen
Present	1st Person	haga	hagamos
Subjunctive	2nd Person *(fam.)*	hagas	hagáis
	3rd Person, 2nd *(form.)*	haga	hagan
Preterite	1st Person	hice	hicimos
	2nd Person *(fam.)*	hiciste	hicisteis
	3rd Person, 2nd *(form.)*	hizo	hicieron
Imperfect	1st Person	hacía	hacíamos
Indicative	2nd Person *(fam.)*	hacías	hacíais
	3rd Person, 2nd *(form.)*	hacía	hacían
Imperfect	1st Person	hiciera	hiciéramos
Subjunctive	2nd Person *(fam.)*	hicieras	hicierais
	3rd Person, 2nd *(form.)*	hiciera	hicieran
Future	1st Person	haré	haremos
	2nd Person *(fam.)*	harás	haréis
	3rd Person, 2nd *(form.)*	hará	harán
Conditional	1st Person	haría	haríamos
	2nd Person *(fam.)*	harías	haríais
	3rd Person, 2nd *(form.)*	haría	harían

Imperative	*Singular*	*Negative*	*Plural*
Formal Command	haga	no haga	} hagan
Familiar Command	haz	no hagas	

Present Participle	haciendo
Past Participle	hecho

IR(SE) TO GO (GO AWAY)

		Singular	Plural
Present Indicative	1st Person	voy	vamos
	2nd Person *(fam.)*	vas	vais
	3rd Person, 2nd *(form.)*	va	van
Present Subjunctive	1st Person	vaya	vayamos
	2nd Person *(fam.)*	vayas	vayáis
	3rd Person, 2nd *(form.)*	vaya	vayan
Preterite	1st Person	fui	fuimos
	2nd Person *(fam.)*	fuiste	fuisteis
	3rd Person, 2nd *(form.)*	fue	fueron
Imperfect Indicative	1st Person	iba	íbamos
	2nd Person *(fam.)*	ibas	ibais
	3rd Person, 2nd *(form.)*	iba	iban
Imperfect Subjunctive	1st Person	fuera	fuéramos
	2nd Person *(fam.)*	fueras	fuerais
	3rd Person, 2nd *(form.)*	fuera	fueran
Future	1st Person	iré	iremos
	2nd Person *(fam.)*	irás	iréis
	3rd Person, 2nd *(form.)*	irá	irán
Conditional	1st Person	iría	iríamos
	2nd Person *(fam.)*	irías	iríais
	3rd Person, 2nd *(form.)*	iría	irían

Imperative	Singular	Negative	Plural
Formal Command	vaya	no vaya	} vayan
Familiar Command	ve	no vayas	
Present Participle	yendo		
Past Participle	ido		

JUGAR TO PLAY

		Singular	*Plural*
Present	1st Person	**juego**	**jugamos**
Indicative	2nd Person *(fam.)*	**juegas**	**jugáis**
	3rd Person, 2nd *(form.)*	**juega**	**juegan**
Present	1st Person	**juegue**	**juguemos**
Subjunctive	2nd Person *(fam.)*	**juegues**	**juguéis**
	3rd Person, 2nd *(form.)*	**juegue**	**jueguen**
Preterite	1st Person	**jugué**	**jugamos**
	2nd Person *(fam.)*	**jugaste**	**jugasteis**
	3rd Person, 2nd *(form.)*	**jugó**	**jugaron**
Imperfect	1st Person	**jugaba**	**jugábamos**
Indicative	2nd Person *(fam.)*	**jugabas**	**jugabais**
	3rd Person, 2nd *(form.)*	**jugaba**	**jugaban**
Imperfect	1st Person	**jugara**	**jugáramos**
Subjunctive	2nd Person *(fam.)*	**jugaras**	**jugarais**
	3rd Person, 2nd *(form.)*	**jugara**	**jugaran**
Future	1st Person	**jugaré**	**jugaremos**
	2nd Person *(fam.)*	**jugarás**	**jugaréis**
	3rd Person, 2nd *(form.)*	**jugará**	**jugarán**
Conditional	1st Person	**jugaría**	**jugaríamos**
	2nd Person *(fam.)*	**jugarías**	**jugaríais**
	3rd Person, 2nd *(form.)*	**jugaría**	**jugarían**

Imperative	*Singular*	*Negative*	*Plural*
Formal Command	**juegue**	**no juegue**	} **jueguen**
Familiar Command	**juega**	**no juegues**	

Present Participle	**jugando**
Past Participle	**jugado**

LEER TO READ

		Singular	*Plural*
Present	1st Person	leo	leemos
Indicative	2nd Person *(fam.)*	lees	leéis
	3rd Person, 2nd *(form.)*	lee	leen
Present	1st Person	lea	leamos
Subjunctive	2nd Person *(fam.)*	leas	leáis
	3rd Person, 2nd *(form.)*	lea	lean
Preterite	1st Person	leí	leímos
	2nd Person *(fam.)*	leíste	leísteis
	3rd Person, 2nd *(form.)*	leyó	leyeron
Imperfect	1st Person	leía	leíamos
Indicative	2nd Person *(fam.)*	leías	leíais
	3rd Person, 2nd *(form.)*	leía	leían
Imperfect	1st Person	leyera	leyéramos
Subjunctive	2nd Person *(fam.)*	leyeras	leyerais
	3rd Person, 2nd *(form.)*	leyera	leyeran
Future	1st Person	leeré	leeremos
	2nd Person *(fam.)*	leerás	leeréis
	3rd Person, 2nd *(form.)*	leerá	leerán
Conditional	1st Person	leería	leeríamos
	2nd Person *(fam.)*	leerías	leeríais
	3rd Person, 2nd *(form.)*	leería	leerían

Imperative	*Singular*	*Negative*	*Plural*
Formal Command	lea	no lea	} lean
Familiar Command	lee	no leas	

Present Participle	leyendo
Past Participle	leído

MOSTRAR TO SHOW

		Singular	*Plural*
Present	1st Person	**muestro**	**mostramos**
Indicative	2nd Person *(fam.)*	**muestras**	**mostráis**
	3rd Person, 2nd *(form.)*	**muestra**	**muestran**
Present	1st Person	**muestre**	**mostremos**
Subjunctive	2nd Person *(fam.)*	**muestres**	**mostréis**
	3rd Person, 2nd *(form.)*	**muestre**	**muestren**
Preterite	1st Person	**mostré**	**mostramos**
	2nd Person *(fam.)*	**mostraste**	**mostrasteis**
	3rd Person, 2nd *(form.)*	**mostró**	**mostraron**
Imperfect	1st Person	**mostraba**	**mostrábamos**
Indicative	2nd Person *(fam.)*	**mostrabas**	**mostrabais**
	3rd Person, 2nd *(form.)*	**mostraba**	**mostraban**
Imperfect	1st Person	**mostrara**	**mostráramos**
Subjunctive	2nd Person *(fam.)*	**mostraras**	**mostrarais**
	3rd Person, 2nd *(form.)*	**mostrara**	**mostraran**
Future	1st Person	**mostraré**	**mostraremos**
	2nd Person *(fam.)*	**mostrarás**	**mostraréis**
	3rd Person, 2nd *(form.)*	**mostrará**	**mostrarán**
Conditional	1st Person	**mostraría**	**mostraríamos**
	2nd Person *(fam.)*	**mostrarías**	**mostraríais**
	3rd Person, 2nd *(form.)*	**mostraría**	**mostrarían**

Imperative	*Singular*	*Negative*	*Plural*
Formal Command	**muestre**	**no muestre**	⎱ **muestren**
Familiar Command	**muestra**	**no muestres**	⎰
Present Participle	**mostrando**		
Past Participle	**mostrado**		

PEDIR TO ASK FOR

		Singular	*Plural*
Present **Indicative**	1st Person	pido	pedimos
	2nd Person *(fam.)*	pides	pedís
	3rd Person, 2nd *(form.)*	pide	piden
Present **Subjunctive**	1st Person	pida	pidamos
	2nd Person *(fam.)*	pidas	pidáis
	3rd Person, 2nd *(form.)*	pida	pidan
Preterite	1st Person	pedí	pedimos
	2nd Person *(fam.)*	pediste	pedisteis
	3rd Person, 2nd *(form.)*	pidió	pidieron
Imperfect **Indicative**	1st Person	pedía	pedíamos
	2nd Person *(fam.)*	pedías	pedíais
	3rd Person, 2nd *(form.)*	pedía	pedían
Imperfect **Subjunctive**	1st Person	pidiera	pidiéramos
	2nd Person *(fam.)*	pidieras	pidierais
	3rd Person, 2nd *(form.)*	pidiera	pidieran
Future	1st Person	pediré	pediremos
	2nd Person *(fam.)*	pedirás	pediréis
	3rd Person, 2nd *(form.)*	pedirá	pedirán
Conditional	1st Person	pediría	pediríamos
	2nd Person *(fam.)*	pedirías	pediríais
	3rd Person, 2nd *(form.)*	pediría	pedirían

Imperative	*Singular*	*Negative*	*Plural*
Formal Command	pida	no pida	} pidan
Familiar Command	pide	no pidas	

Present Participle	pidiendo
Past Participle	pedido

PENSAR TO THINK

		Singular	*Plural*
Present **Indicative**	1st Person	**pienso**	**pensamos**
	2nd Person *(fam.)*	**piensas**	**pensáis**
	3rd Person, 2nd *(form.)*	**piensa**	**piensan**
Present **Subjunctive**	1st Person	**piense**	**pensemos**
	2nd Person *(fam.)*	**pienses**	**penséis**
	3rd Person, 2nd *(form.)*	**piense**	**piensen**
Preterite	1st Person	**pensé**	**pensamos**
	2nd Person *(fam.)*	**pensaste**	**pensasteis**
	3rd Person, 2nd *(form.)*	**pensó**	**pensaron**
Imperfect **Indicative**	1st Person	**pensaba**	**pensábamos**
	2nd Person *(fam.)*	**pensabas**	**pensabais**
	3rd Person, 2nd *(form.)*	**pensaba**	**pensaban**
Imperfect **Subjunctive**	1st Person	**pensara**	**pensáramos**
	2nd Person *(fam.)*	**pensaras**	**pensarais**
	3rd Person, 2nd *(form.)*	**pensara**	**pensaran**
Future	1st Person	**pensaré**	**pensaremos**
	2nd Person *(fam.)*	**pensarás**	**pensaréis**
	3rd Person, 2nd *(form.)*	**pensará**	**pensarán**
Conditional	1st Person	**pensaría**	**pensaríamos**
	2nd Person *(fam.)*	**pensarías**	**pensaríais**
	3rd Person, 2nd *(form.)*	**pensaría**	**pensarían**

Imperative	*Singular*	*Negative*	*Plural*
Formal Command	**piense**	**no piense**	} **piensen**
Familiar Command	**piensa**	**no pienses**	
Present Participle	**pensando**		
Past Participle	**pensado**		

PODER TO BE ABLE

		Singular	*Plural*
Present	1st Person	**puedo**	**podemos**
Indicative	2nd Person *(fam.)*	**puedes**	**podéis**
	3rd Person, 2nd *(form.)*	**puede**	**pueden**
Present	1st Person	**pueda**	**podamos**
Subjunctive	2nd Person *(fam.)*	**puedas**	**podáis**
	3rd Person, 2nd *(form.)*	**pueda**	**puedan**
Preterite	1st Person	**pude**	**pudimos**
	2nd Person *(fam.)*	**pudiste**	**pudisteis**
	3rd Person, 2nd *(form.)*	**pudo**	**pudieron**
Imperfect	1st Person	**podía**	**podíamos**
Indicative	2nd Person *(fam.)*	**podías**	**podíais**
	3rd Person, 2nd *(form.)*	**podía**	**podían**
Imperfect	1st Person	**pudiera**	**pudiéramos**
Subjunctive	2nd Person *(fam.)*	**pudieras**	**pudierais**
	3rd Person, 2nd *(form.)*	**pudiera**	**pudieran**
Future	1st Person	**podré**	**podremos**
	2nd Person *(fam.)*	**podrás**	**podréis**
	3rd Person, 2nd *(form.)*	**podrá**	**podrán**
Conditional	1st Person	**podría**	**podríamos**
	2nd Person *(fam.)*	**podrías**	**podríais**
	3rd Person, 2nd *(form.)*	**podría**	**podrían**

Imperative	*Singular*	*Negative*	*Plural*

Formal Command
} (not applicable)
Familiar Command

Present Participle   **pudiendo**

Past Participle   **podido**

PONER TO PUT, PLACE

		Singular	*Plural*
Present **Indicative**	1st Person	**pongo**	**ponemos**
	2nd Person *(fam.)*	**pones**	**ponéis**
	3rd Person, 2nd *(form.)*	**pone**	**ponen**
Present **Subjunctive**	1st Person	**ponga**	**pongamos**
	2nd Person *(fam.)*	**pongas**	**pongáis**
	3rd Person, 2nd *(form.)*	**ponga**	**pongan**
Preterite	1st Person	**puse**	**pusimos**
	2nd Person *(fam.)*	**pusiste**	**pusisteis**
	3rd Person, 2nd *(form.)*	**puso**	**pusieron**
Imperfect **Indicative**	1st Person	**ponía**	**poníamos**
	2nd Person *(fam.)*	**ponías**	**poníais**
	3rd Person, 2nd *(form.)*	**ponía**	**ponían**
Imperfect **Subjunctive**	1st Person	**pusiera**	**pusiéramos**
	2nd Person *(fam.)*	**pusieras**	**pusierais**
	3rd Person, 2nd *(form.)*	**pusiera**	**pusieran**
Future	1st Person	**pondré**	**pondremos**
	2nd Person *(fam.)*	**pondrás**	**pondréis**
	3rd Person, 2nd *(form.)*	**pondrá**	**pondrán**
Conditional	1st Person	**pondría**	**pondríamos**
	2nd Person *(fam.)*	**pondrías**	**pondríais**
	3rd Person, 2nd *(form.)*	**pondría**	**pondrían**

Imperative	*Singular*	*Negative*	*Plural*
Formal Command	**ponga**	**no ponga**	⎫ **pongan**
Familiar Command	**pon**	**no pongas**	⎭
Present Participle	**poniendo**		
Past Participle	**puesto**		

QUERER TO WANT, LOVE

		Singular	*Plural*
Present	1st Person	quiero	queremos
Indicative	2nd Person *(fam.)*	quieres	queréis
	3rd Person, 2nd *(form.)*	quiere	quieren
Present	1st Person	quiera	queramos
Subjunctive	2nd Person *(fam.)*	quieras	queráis
	3rd Person, 2nd *(form.)*	quiera	quieran
Preterite	1st Person	quise	quisimos
	2nd Person *(fam.)*	quisiste	quisisteis
	3rd Person, 2nd *(form.)*	quiso	quisieron
Imperfect	1st Person	quería	queríamos
Indicative	2nd Person *(fam.)*	querías	queríais
	3rd Person, 2nd *(form.)*	quería	querían
Imperfect	1st Person	quisiera	quisiéramos
Subjunctive	2nd Person *(fam.)*	quisieras	quisierais
	3rd Person, 2nd *(form.)*	quisiera	quisieran
Future	1st Person	querré	querremos
	2nd Person *(fam.)*	querrás	querréis
	3rd Person, 2nd *(form.)*	querrá	querrán
Conditional	1st Person	querría	querríamos
	2nd Person *(fam.)*	querrías	querríais
	3rd Person, 2nd *(form.)*	querría	querrían

Imperative	*Singular*	*Negative*	*Plural*
Formal Command	quiera	no quiera	} quieran
Familiar Command	quiere	no quieras	

Present Participle	queriendo
Past Participle	querido

SABER TO KNOW

		Singular	Plural
Present	1st Person	sé	sabemos
Indicative	2nd Person *(fam.)*	sabes	sabéis
	3rd Person, 2nd *(form.)*	sabe	saben
Present	1st Person	sepa	sepamos
Subjunctive	2nd Person *(fam.)*	sepas	sepáis
	3rd Person, 2nd *(form.)*	sepa	sepan
Preterite	1st Person	supe	supimos
	2nd Person *(fam.)*	supiste	supisteis
	3rd Person, 2nd *(form.)*	supo	supieron
Imperfect	1st Person	sabía	sabíamos
Indicative	2nd Person *(fam.)*	sabías	sabíais
	3rd Person, 2nd *(form.)*	sabía	sabían
Imperfect	1st Person	supiera	supiéramos
Subjunctive	2nd Person *(fam.)*	supieras	supierais
	3rd Person, 2nd *(form.)*	supiera	supieran
Future	1st Person	sabré	sabremos
	2nd Person *(fam.)*	sabrás	sabréis
	3rd Person, 2nd *(form.)*	sabrá	sabrán
Conditional	1st Person	sabría	sabríamos
	2nd Person *(fam.)*	sabrías	sabríais
	3rd Person, 2nd *(form.)*	sabría	sabrían

Imperative	Singular	Negative	Plural
Formal Command	sepa	no sepa	} sepan
Familiar Command	sabe	no sepas	
Present Participle	sabiendo		
Past Participle	sabido		

SALIR TO LEAVE

		Singular	Plural
Present	1st Person	**salgo**	**salimos**
Indicative	2nd Person *(fam.)*	**sales**	**salís**
	3rd Person, 2nd *(form.)*	**sale**	**salen**
Present	1st Person	**salga**	**salgamos**
Subjunctive	2nd Person *(fam.)*	**salgas**	**salgáis**
	3rd Person, 2nd *(form.)*	**salga**	**salgan**
Preterite	1st Person	**salí**	**salimos**
	2nd Person *(fam.)*	**saliste**	**salisteis**
	3rd Person, 2nd *(form.)*	**salió**	**salieron**
Imperfect	1st Person	**salía**	**salíamos**
Indicative	2nd Person *(fam.)*	**salías**	**salíais**
	3rd Person, 2nd *(form.)*	**salía**	**salían**
Imperfect	1st Person	**saliera**	**saliéramos**
Subjunctive	2nd Person *(fam.)*	**salieras**	**salierais**
	3rd Person, 2nd *(form.)*	**saliera**	**salieran**
Future	1st Person	**saldré**	**saldremos**
	2nd Person *(fam.)*	**saldrás**	**saldréis**
	3rd Person, 2nd *(form.)*	**saldrá**	**saldrán**
Conditional	1st Person	**saldría**	**saldríamos**
	2nd Person *(fam.)*	**saldrías**	**saldríais**
	3rd Person, 2nd *(form.)*	**saldría**	**saldrían**

Imperative	Singular	Negative	Plural
Formal Command	**salga**	**no salga**	} **salgan**
Familiar Command	**sal**	**no salgas**	
Present Participle	**saliendo**		
Past Participle	**salido**		

SER TO BE

		Singular	*Plural*
Present	1st Person	**soy**	**somos**
Indicative	2nd Person *(fam.)*	**eres**	**sois**
	3rd Person, 2nd *(form.)*	**es**	**son**
Present	1st Person	**sea**	**seamos**
Subjunctive	2nd Person *(fam.)*	**seas**	**seáis**
	3rd Person, 2nd *(form.)*	**sea**	**sean**
Preterite	1st Person	**fui**	**fuimos**
	2nd Person *(fam.)*	**fuiste**	**fuisteis**
	3rd Person, 2nd *(form.)*	**fue**	**fueron**
Imperfect	1st Person	**era**	**éramos**
Indicative	2nd Person *(fam.)*	**eras**	**erais**
	3rd Person, 2nd *(form.)*	**era**	**eran**
Imperfect	1st Person	**fuera**	**fuéramos**
Subjunctive	2nd Person *(fam.)*	**fueras**	**fuerais**
	3rd Person, 2nd *(form.)*	**fuera**	**fueran**
Future	1st Person	**seré**	**seremos**
	2nd Person *(fam.)*	**serás**	**seréis**
	3rd Person, 2nd *(form.)*	**será**	**serán**
Conditional	1st Person	**sería**	**seríamos**
	2nd Person *(fam.)*	**serías**	**seríais**
	3rd Person, 2nd *(form.)*	**sería**	**serían**

Imperative	*Singular*	*Negative*	*Plural*
Formal Command	**sea**	**no sea**	} **sean**
Familiar Command	**sé**	**no seas**	
Present Participle	**siendo**		
Past Participle	**sido**		

TENER TO HAVE

		Singular	*Plural*
Present	1st Person	**tengo**	**tenemos**
Indicative	2nd Person *(fam.)*	**tienes**	**tenéis**
	3rd Person, 2nd *(form.)*	**tiene**	**tienen**
Present	1st Person	**tenga**	**tengamos**
Subjunctive	2nd Person *(fam.)*	**tengas**	**tengáis**
	3rd Person, 2nd *(form.)*	**tenga**	**tengan**
Preterite	1st Person	**tuve**	**tuvimos**
	2nd Person *(fam.)*	**tuviste**	**tuvisteis**
	3rd Person, 2nd *(form.)*	**tuvo**	**tuvieron**
Imperfect	1st Person	**tenía**	**teníamos**
Indicative	2nd Person *(fam.)*	**tenías**	**teníais**
	3rd Person, 2nd *(form.)*	**tenía**	**tenían**
Imperfect	1st Person	**tuviera**	**tuviéramos**
Subjunctive	2nd Person *(fam.)*	**tuvieras**	**tuvierais**
	3rd Person, 2nd *(form.)*	**tuviera**	**tuvieran**
Future	1st Person	**tendré**	**tendremos**
	2nd Person *(fam.)*	**tendrás**	**tendréis**
	3rd Person, 2nd *(form.)*	**tendrá**	**tendrán**
Conditional	1st Person	**tendría**	**tendríamos**
	2nd Person *(fam.)*	**tendrías**	**tendríais**
	3rd Person, 2nd *(form.)*	**tendría**	**tendrían**

Imperative	*Singular*	*Negative*	*Plural*
Formal Command	**tenga**	**no tenga**	} **tengan**
Familiar Command	**ten**	**no tengas**	
Present Participle	**teniendo**		
Past Participle	**tenido**		

TRAER TO BRING

		Singular	*Plural*
Present	1st Person	**traigo**	**traemos**
Indicative	2nd Person *(fam.)*	**traes**	**traéis**
	3rd Person, 2nd *(form.)*	**trae**	**traen**
Present	1st Person	**traiga**	**traigamos**
Subjunctive	2nd Person *(fam.)*	**traigas**	**traigáis**
	3rd Person, 2nd *(form.)*	**traiga**	**traigan**
Preterite	1st Person	**traje**	**trajimos**
	2nd Person *(fam.)*	**trajiste**	**trajisteis**
	3rd Person, 2nd *(form.)*	**trajo**	**trajeron**
Imperfect	1st Person	**traía**	**traíamos**
Indicative	2nd Person *(fam.)*	**traías**	**traíais**
	3rd Person, 2nd *(form.)*	**traía**	**traían**
Imperfect	1st Person	**trajera**	**trajéramos**
Subjunctive	2nd Person *(fam.)*	**trajeras**	**trajerais**
	3rd Person, 2nd *(form.)*	**trajera**	**trajeran**
Future	1st Person	**traeré**	**traeremos**
	2nd Person *(fam.)*	**traerás**	**traeréis**
	3rd Person, 2nd *(form.)*	**traerá**	**traerán**
Conditional	1st Person	**traería**	**traeríamos**
	2nd Person *(fam.)*	**traerías**	**traeríais**
	3rd Person, 2nd *(form.)*	**traería**	**traerían**

Imperative	*Singular*	*Negative*	*Plural*
Formal Command	traiga	no traiga	} **traigan**
Familiar Command	trae	no traigas	
Present Participle	trayendo		
Past Participle	traído		

VENIR TO COME

		Singular	*Plural*
Present	1st Person	**vengo**	**venimos**
Indicative	2nd Person *(fam.)*	**vienes**	**venís**
	3rd Person, 2nd *(form.)*	**viene**	**vienen**
Present	1st Person	**venga**	**vengamos**
Subjunctive	2nd Person *(fam.)*	**vengas**	**vengáis**
	3rd Person, 2nd *(form.)*	**venga**	**vengan**
Preterite	1st Person	**vine**	**vinimos**
	2nd Person *(fam.)*	**viniste**	**vinisteis**
	3rd Person, 2nd *(form.)*	**vino**	**vinieron**
Imperfect	1st Person	**venía**	**veníamos**
Indicative	2nd Person *(fam.)*	**venías**	**veníais**
	3rd Person, 2nd *(form.)*	**venía**	**venían**
Imperfect	1st Person	**viniera**	**viniéramos**
Subjunctive	2nd Person *(fam.)*	**vinieras**	**vinierais**
	3rd Person, 2nd *(form.)*	**viniera**	**vinieran**
Future	1st Person	**vendré**	**vendremos**
	2nd Person *(fam.)*	**vendrás**	**vendréis**
	3rd Person, 2nd *(form.)*	**vendrá**	**vendrán**
Conditional	1st Person	**vendría**	**vendríamos**
	2nd Person *(fam.)*	**vendrías**	**vendríais**
	3rd Person, 2nd *(form.)*	**vendría**	**vendrían**

Imperative	*Singular*	*Negative*	*Plural*
Formal Command	**venga**	**no venga**	} **vengan**
Familiar Command	**ven**	**no vengas**	
Present Participle	**viniendo**		
Past Participle	**venido**		

VER TO SEE

		Singular	*Plural*
Present	1st Person	**veo**	**vemos**
Indicative	2nd Person *(fam.)*	**ves**	**veis**
	3rd Person, 2nd *(form.)*	**ve**	**ven**
Present	1st Person	**vea**	**veamos**
Subjunctive	2nd Person *(fam.)*	**veas**	**veáis**
	3rd Person, 2nd *(form.)*	**vea**	**vean**
Preterite	1st Person	**vi**	**vimos**
	2nd Person *(fam.)*	**viste**	**visteis**
	3rd Person, 2nd *(form.)*	**vio**	**vieron**
Imperfect	1st Person	**veía**	**veíamos**
Indicative	2nd Person *(fam.)*	**veías**	**veíais**
	3rd Person, 2nd *(form.)*	**veía**	**veían**
Imperfect	1st Person	**viera**	**viéramos**
Subjunctive	2nd Person *(fam.)*	**vieras**	**vierais**
	3rd Person, 2nd *(form.)*	**viera**	**vieran**
Future	1st Person	**veré**	**veremos**
	2nd Person *(fam.)*	**verás**	**veréis**
	3rd Person, 2nd *(form.)*	**verá**	**verán**
Conditional	1st Person	**vería**	**veríamos**
	2nd Person *(fam.)*	**verías**	**veríais**
	3rd Person, 2nd *(form.)*	**vería**	**verían**

Imperative	*Singular*	*Negative*	*Plural*
Formal Command	**vea**	**no vea**	} **vean**
Familiar Command	**ve**	**no veas**	

Present Participle	**viendo**
Past Participle	**visto**

VIVIR TO LIVE *(REGULAR -IR)*

		Singular	*Plural*
Present	1st Person	vivo	vivimos
Indicative	2nd Person *(fam.)*	vives	vivís
	3rd Person, 2nd *(form.)*	vive	viven
Present	1st Person	viva	vivamos
Subjunctive	2nd Person *(fam.)*	vivas	viváis
	3rd Person, 2nd *(form.)*	viva	vivan
Preterite	1st Person	viví	vivimos
	2nd Person *(fam.)*	viviste	vivisteis
	3rd Person, 2nd *(form.)*	vivió	vivieron
Imperfect	1st Person	vivía	vivíamos
Indicative	2nd Person *(fam.)*	vivías	vivíais
	3rd Person, 2nd *(form.)*	vivía	vivían
Imperfect	1st Person	viviera	viviéramos
Subjunctive	2nd Person *(fam.)*	vivieras	vivierais
	3rd Person, 2nd *(form.)*	viviera	vivieran
Future	1st Person	viviré	viviremos
	2nd Person *(fam.)*	vivirás	viviréis
	3rd Person, 2nd *(form.)*	vivirá	vivirán
Conditional	1st Person	viviría	viviríamos
	2nd Person *(fam.)*	vivirías	viviríais
	3rd Person, 2nd *(form.)*	viviría	vivirían

Imperative	*Singular*	*Negative*	*Plural*
Formal Command	viva	no viva	} vivan
Familiar Command	vive	no vivas	
Present Participle	viviendo		
Past Participle	vivido		

Index